Visitor's Guide to the Bahamas

Grand Bahama Island & Freeport

Copyright © 2013.

By
Blair Howard

This guide focuses on recreational activities. As all such activities contain elements of risk, the publisher, author, affiliated individuals and companies disclaim responsibility for any injury, harm, or illness that may occur to anyone through, or by use of, the information in this book. Every effort was made to insure the accuracy of information in this book, but the publisher and author do not assume, and hereby disclaim, liability for any loss or damage caused by errors, omissions, misleading information or potential travel problems caused by this guide, even if such errors or omissions result from negligence, accident or any other cause.

Important Note: The rates, fees and prices, and especially the entrance fees to the many attractions, quoted throughout this book were current at the time of writing. However, they are all subject to change without notice and they do, almost weekly, thus the prices quoted herein are given only as a rough guide as to what you might expect to pay. The author therefore disclaims any liability for such changes and urges you to check, either by phone or online for current rates before you travel.

Planning a visit to Grand Bahama Island?

If so, you'll find this book to be an invaluable guide. Everything you need to know to plan your visit is included.

This guide includes up-to-date information about the best hotels, attractions, things to do, touring the islands, restaurants, the beaches, snorkeling, guided tours, hiking, dive sites, dive operators, fishing guides and much more.

The book also includes up-to-date practical information: everything you need to know to make your visit to Grand Bahama Island a success.

The Visitor's Guide to the Bahamas – Grand Bahama Island & Freeport is the most complete travel guide to the islands available.

Contents

Grand Bahama Island is home to the second largest city in the Bahamas, Freeport, and is, in every sense of the description, the younger sister island to New Providence and Nassau. Through the efforts of some seriously dedicated institutions, including The Lucayan national Park System and the Rand Memorial Nature Center (two must-visits), Grand Bahama Island has become the environmental center for the Bahamas.

Grand Bahama Island itself is not so hectic and busy as its bigger sister to the south. Beyond Freeport and Lucaya, the island reverts to the timeless beauty of the Out Islands, long dusty roads, quiet beaches, tiny fishing villages where time seems to have stood still: East End did not get electricity until the 1980s. Beyond Freeport and Lucaya, the island is an almost deserted paradise, little known by the outside, and rarely visited, even the locals in the larger population centers on the island.

Freeport and Lucaya are the main population centers for the island. It's here you'll find the large resort hotels, golf courses, casinos, miles of sandy beaches, a waterfront district with lots of restaurants and opportunities for shopping. Talking of casinos, only one is open at the time of this writing; the Royal Oasis Golf Resort & Casino has been closed for some time. The other one, though not on the grand scale of the massive offering at Atlantis on Paradise Island, Treasure Bay Casino at Our Lucaya, is a 35,000 square foot facility that provides non-stop gambling fun and excitement, if you like that sort of thing.

Grand Bahama is just 50 miles from Florida's east coast, and less than 30 minutes by air. The island's main population area is a small world of cosmopolitan glitz and glamour, while the outlying areas are virtually deserted: miles of "pristine beaches and endless turquoise seas" are part of an unexplored world of beauty and utter relaxation.

The main population center is the **Freeport/Lucaya** area, a modern, well-planned urban metropolis where some 55,000 souls live and spend their days in quiet harmony. Freeport is the economic center for the island. It's also the hub of activity for visitors who arrive daily by air, cruise ship and private boat. Sightseeing, shopping, gambling, watersports, golf, tennis and seemingly never-ending sunshine are just a few of the attractions.

Grand Bahama is surrounded by crystal-clear emerald seas, sugar-white beaches, and spectacular coral reefs. You can dive with and feed sharks, or spend a quiet moment in the soothing company of an Atlantic bottlenose dolphin. You can, after a week of instruction, become a fully certified diver. If that sounds a little too much, after just three hours of

instruction, you can take to the deep sea –
complete with fins, tanks, and weights – for an
underwater experience you'll never forget. Too
old? Nonsense! It's never too late.

Golfers are in for a rare treat. There are four
golf courses on the island – among the best
courses in the Caribbean: unfortunately two are
not open for play - the PGA-rated Ruby and
Emerald courses at the one-time Royal Oasis Golf
Resort & Casino, But the two courses at Our
Lucaya, The Reefs and The Lucayan are both
open for play and will provide a nice challenge
and a memorable experience.

If shopping appeals to you, head for **Port
Lucaya**, where more than six acres of shopping,
dining, and entertainment await you at The
Marketplace.

In downtown **Freeport**, you'll find more than 90 shops and stores in the International Bazaar. And the Straw Market just next door is a treasure house of crafts and specialties.

Aside from the ocean and beaches that teem with life, there's also the unique Lucayan National Park, the magnificent Botanical Gardens, and the Rand Memorial Nature Center, and one of the world's largest underwater cave systems, all of which are devoted to preservation of the island's ecology and its wildlife. Throughout these three centers, dozens of nature trails and woodland paths meander back and forth among the mangrove swamps, flower gardens, and forests. For those who really like to get away into the outback, there are more than 90 miles of virtually untouched wilderness and deserted shores to explore – a world of casuarina, seagrape, mangrove, palmetto, seagrass, and scrub, where buzzards, lizards, and crabs, along with a fisherman or two, live out the great cycle of life.

Better yet, a day-long safari to the far ends of the island will provide you with an experience you're never likely to forget: the villagers in the tiny communities of **West End** and **McClean's Town** will extend a warm welcome and create some of the finest Bahamian cuisine you'll ever taste.

Smiling Pat

For almost 300 years of its early in its history, Grand Bahama was virtually uninhabited. Then, with the development of Freeport/Lucaya in the

1950s, and because of the island's close proximity to Florida's east coast, it is now one of the most visited of all the Bahamian islands.

Grand Bahama and Freeport make for a unique destination; visitors can combine a cosmopolitan vacation at a world-class resort with the charm of the old-world, tiny coastal villages and ecological treasures as yet unspoiled. Grand Bahama offers a wide variety of accommodations, from sprawling deluxe resorts to the beachfront hotels, self-catering apartments, secluded getaways inns and small economy hotels. The island is one of my own personal favorite getaways: it's easy to get to, the weather's always good, the golf spectacular, the accommodations comfortable, and the people are friendly and welcoming. What more could you want?

History

Grand Bahama is the fourth-largest of the Bahamian islands, and Freeport is the second largest city. While the island has been inhabited throughout recorded history, its modern history began in the 1950s with the development of Freeport and Lucaya.

The first inhabitants of the islands were **Stone-Age Indians** from Cuba. They were replaced almost 1,000 years ago by the **Lucayans**. They, in turn, were displaced and pretty well exterminated with the arrival of the Europeans shortly after Columbus discovered the islands in 1492. From then on, Grand Bahama was the forgotten island of the Bahamas. Except for the occasional band of pirates or loyalists, it remained virtually uninhabited for almost 300 years.

Grand Bahama was given its name by the Spanish – "gran bajamar" means "great shallows" – for the vast reaches of flats and shoals in the waters off the island.

The first permanent settlers arrived during the late 19th century. Most of them scratched out a living from the sea as fishermen, or by harvesting the abundant timber from the land. During the American Civil War, the small population declined even further when people began abandoning their farms and flocked to Nassau to join the economic boom brought by the blockade runners. Prohibition in America during the 1920s created something of a mini-boom in the island's economy when the rumrunners moved in. But the new prosperity was short-lived.

In 1955, American financier **Wallace Groves**, who had extensive lumber interests on the island, made a proposal to the Bahamian government to build a tax-free city on Grand Bahama. In return, Groves would be granted tax exemptions and exclusive development rights. His proposal was accepted, and modern Freeport is the result. Groves also built the resort city of Lucaya, just five miles south of Freeport. His innovations attracted more investors to the island and, between

1963 and 1967, investment, along with the population of Grand Bahama, more than tripled.

Today on Grand Bahama, as everywhere else in the islands, tourism is king. Every year thousands upon thousands of tourists visit to take advantage of its many attractions and its tax-free status.

Important Note:

Most of the practical information applies to Grand Bahama Island and New Providence Island (Nassau). It seemed prudent to include it all here.

Travel Documents

To enter the Bahamas you'll need two things: a return or onward-bound ticket and a valid passport. A visa is not required. US immigration officials will want to see proof of US citizenship on your return. See the State Department website for details at http://travel.state.gov/bahamas.html.

Canadian and British citizens visiting for three weeks or less may enter by showing the same documents as required for US citizens. Citizens of British Commonwealth countries do not need visas.

Customs

Dutiable items, such as furniture, china and linens, must be declared. Each adult may bring in duty-free 200 cigarettes, or 50 cigars or one pound of tobacco and one quart of alcohol.

US residents, including children, may take home duty-free purchases valued up to $800, and up to 67 ounces of alcohol per person over the age of 21. Canadian citizens may take home up to $200 in purchases, including up to 200 cigarettes,

50 cigars, two lbs of tobacco and 40 oz of alcohol. Residents of Great Britain may take home up to £32 in duty-free purchases and each adult visitor is allowed 200 cigarettes or 50 cigars or one pound of tobacco and a liter of alcohol without paying duty.

Departure Taxes

At the time of writing, the government departure tax of $15 is included in the cost of most airline tickets. Children under six are exempt. There is an additional $10 security fee for international passengers departing from Freeport, Grand Bahama.

Disabled Travelers

If you're disabled, or traveling with someone who is disabled, make all your arrangements well in advance. Be sure that you let everyone involved know the nature of the disability so that accommodations and facilities can be arranged to meet your needs. On the whole, you'll find most hotels, tour operators, and other facilities are well equipped to handle the needs of disabled visitors.

The People

The Bahamas, still very much steeped in their traditional British heritage, are inhabited by a hodgepodge of black and white races of African-American, Continental European, and African origin, among others. Less than 40 years ago, blacks on the islands were not allowed in any of the nation's restaurants, theaters, and hotels, although they represented more than 80Phoneof the population. That is all changed now and, although several islands remain predominantly white, Bahamians of all colors integrate freely with one another.

With independence from Britain in 1973, and with tourism becoming the mainstay of the Bahamian economy, black people, once the poorest members of the population, have increasingly improved their lot.

The bulk of the wealth is still in white hands, but more and more black-owned business are making a contribution. Where once they were not allowed, black Bahamians have found their way into administration and management. And while many young Bahamians still leave the islands in search of something better, it seems most of them return sooner or later.

Bahamians, black or white, are very friendly and outgoing. The always cheerful "good morning," the happy smile, and the eagerness to help, whether it's with directions or service, often borders on the cloying. But rest assured, it's done with an almost naïve genuineness and a desire to please.

Language

The language spoken on the islands is English – at least it's called English. The old language has been shaped and reshaped over more than 300 years by a potpourri of cultures, of which the British and Caribbean have had no small influence. Some say the Bahamian accent is decidedly West Indian, others say it has a sound all its own. If it's spoken quickly, it's almost impossible for an outsider to understand. The secret is to listen carefully, and don't be afraid to ask the speaker to repeat – that will often bring a delighted grin to his or her face.

People to People

If you want to get to know the real Bahamians, go out and meet the people. This is easily achieved through the government-sponsored "People to People" program offered by the Ministry of Tourism. It gives visitors the opportunity to meet and socialize with Bahamians, meeting them in their homes and participating in their social and cultural events. Get involved and you'll be invited to a variety of activities and social events. These might include performances by a local theater group, sporting events, or afternoon tea with a Bahamian family. For more information, contact the People-to-People Unit at the Tourist Information Center at Rawson Square in Nassau, at one of the information booths at the Nassau International Airport, or on Bay Street next to the Straw Market, at Prince George Dock, where the Ministry of Tourism's main office is located. In Freeport, there's a tourist office at the International Bazaar. In the Out Islands there are offices on Abaco, Eleuthera and the Exumas. To find out more on the Internet, go to www.bahamas.com, click on People at the left of the screen, then click on People-to-People Programme.

Eating & Drinking

Bahamian food is an adventure in itself. The larder of the Bahamas is the sea that surrounds it; seafood is the staple.

Feast from the Sea

The conch – pronounced "konk" – is chief among the many varieties of goodies gathered from the ocean. Claimed by the locals to be an aphrodisiac, conch can be prepared in numerous ways: for conch salad the flesh is chopped, spiced, and eaten raw with vegetables and lime juice; cracked conch is beaten and fried; and, finally, there are conch fritters. Be sure to try conch salad before you leave; it's delicious.

Fish, especially grouper, is the principal fare of the Bahamian people. It's served many ways, for breakfast, lunch and dinner. The Bahamian lobster (Americans call it crayfish) is plentiful, often large, and not as expensive as it is in the States. Try minced lobster, a mixture of shredded lobster meat cooked with tomatoes, green peppers and onions, and served in the shell.

Fishy Delights

Fish is prepared in a number of ways, the names of which are often confusing. Boil fish is served for breakfast. It's cooked with salt pork, green peppers and onions, and served with a generous portion of grits. Stew fish is prepared with celery, tomatoes, onions, and spices, all combined in a thick brown gravy; it is also served for breakfast. Steamed fish is cooked in a tomato base and is as tasty as it is novel. And nowhere else will you find anything like this:

Traditional Foods

Bahamians also eat a lot of crab, chicken, pork, and mutton. Almost everything is served with huge portions of peas and rice – a concoction of pigeon peas, peppers, celery, tomatoes, and rice, seasoned and cooked until golden brown.

For dessert, try guava duff, a Bahamian delicacy made by spreading guava fruit pulp on a sheet of dough. It's then rolled and boiled, cut into slices and served with a thick white sauce.

Other than fish, most of the food eaten on the islands is imported, which makes it somewhat expensive. While restaurants on the Out Islands tend to serve mostly Bahamian foods, more and more American fare is making its way onto Bahamian tables. You can find a good steak or prime rib and the inevitable French fries at most of the popular restaurants in Nassau and Freeport. And almost all of the American fast-food chains are represented: McDonalds, Burger King, KFC. There's even a Pizza Hut on Abaco. But to avoid the local food is to miss a great eating experience.

Drinks

Popular drinks are the Bahama Mama, the Goombay Smash, and the Yellow Bird. Bahamians also drink lots and lots of beer, mostly the local brew: a fine golden beer called Kalik. Be sure to try it. Imported beers from America and Europe are also available but, like everything else that has to be imported, they're expensive. For something really different, try one of the locally brewed sodas with exotic names.

All drinks on the islands are expensive. Be prepared to pay up to $7 for a bottle of beer in a restaurant, $7 for cocktails. Even non-alcoholic cocktails kids can consume in large quantities are pricey. A Coke or locally made soda can cost up to $4.

During the day, hot tea is the drink of preference. If you want iced tea, be sure to specify that when ordering. On most of the islands, the water is pure and safe to drink straight from the tap.

Nassau's water is imported from Andros by ship and, by the time it reaches the consumer, the taste is not what you might like. It's best to drink only bottled water in Nassau because of that.

Tipping

It's standard to add a 15% charge to restaurant checks and the same with room service in the large hotels. If you don't see a gratuity on the bill, ask. Hotels add an 8%-10% service charge to their rates, so there's no need to leave a room tip. Tour guides expect to receive $2 to $5 per person, and cab drivers usually receive 10%-15% of the fare.

Accommodations

Hotels on the two main islands, New Providence and Grand Bahama, range in quality from Tourist Class through Superior Deluxe. Remember, however, that you are not dealing with the same standards you have grown used to in the United States, Canada or England. Even the top-rated hotels are almost always busy, and geared to accommodate the vacationing public, rather than business people. In general, this means that, unless you book the best room your particular hotel has to offer, your accommodations will probably be no better than average. Clean and comfortable, yes; luxurious, hardly.

Pelican Bay Resort in Port Lucaya

Hotel Classification Guide

SUPERIOR DELUXE: Exclusive, elegant, luxury hotels offering the highest standards of accommodations, service and facilities.

DELUXE: Outstanding hotels with many of the features and amenities offered by those classed as Superior Deluxe, but less expensive.

SUPERIOR FIRST CLASS: Above-average hotels, often older, but well-maintained.

Accommodations are comfortable and tastefully furnished.

FIRST CLASS: Facilities are not as extensive as those at hotels in the more expensive categories, but these hotels are dependable and comfortable.

SUPERIOR TOURIST CLASS: Budget properties, mostly well-kept and maintained. Facilities are few, but the rooms are generally clean and comfortable, if sometimes spartan.

TOURIST CLASS: Low budget, with few or no facilities. Not for the discriminating traveler.

Package Deals

If your vacation is a package provided by a major operator, you can generally expect your hotel to be clean and comfortable. Package operators inspect their client hotels regularly and require certain minimum standards. This doesn't mean you get better service or accommodations, just that you can be assured of certain standards.

Hotels are listed in order by rate, the least expensive first. Actual rates, when not quoted within the text, are shown at the back of the book in the At a Glance section.

Meal Plans

CP (Continental Plan) includes a continental breakfast.

EP (European Plan) denotes no meals, although restaurant facilities are available either on the property or nearby.

MAP (Modified American Plan) denotes breakfast and dinner.

FAP (Full American Plan) includes all meals.

All-Inc. (All-Inclusive Plan) includes all meals, beverages (alcoholic and soft), watersports, tennis and golf, if available.

All hotel rates quoted are subject to a room tax and a resort levy; gratuities are extra.

Practical Information
Banking

Banking is big business in the Bahamas. Long recognized as a tax haven, both Nassau and Freeport are home to more than their fair share of counting houses. And for visitors to the islands that's good. There's always a bank around the next corner.

In Nassau and Freeport/Lucaya, banks are open from 9:30 am until 3 pm, Monday through Thursday, and from 9:30 am until 5 pm on Friday. If you rely on credit cards for your cash, there are international ATMs located at strategic spots on both of the major islands, including the casinos. As one might expect, banking hours vary in the Out Islands. In fact, banks on some islands open only on certain days of the week, and then only for a few hours.

Bicycles & Mopeds

Bicycles are popular on the islands. Visitors love them. They are inexpensive to rent, convenient, easy to park, and nowhere is really too far away. The only concern is that you'll be riding on the "wrong" side of the road. You can rent mopeds and bicycles at most hotels and resorts, or at nearby cycle shops. At the time or writing, the going rates for mopeds range from about $20 to $30 a day – a half-day might cost anywhere from $10 to $20 – and you'll be asked to leave a small deposit, usually about $30. Bicycles run about $18 a day.

Buses

Bus travel can be an adventure. And if you want to meet the people, there's no better way to do it than finding your way around Nassau by bus. For 75¢, it's a great way to travel. Bahamians are very friendly and will come to your aid quickly with directions. (The only problem is understanding the waving hands and the fast talk.) On Grand Bahama, the buses connect Freeport with Lucaya, the hotels, the beaches, Port Lucaya and, of course, the International Bazaar.

Casinos

Visitors over the age of 18 may gamble at all four casinos in Nassau and Freeport. Children are allowed to enter the casinos only to attend shows in the casino theaters. In Nassau, there is a casino on Paradise Island at the Atlantis Resort and one at Wyndham Nassau Resort & Crystal Palace Casino on Cable Beach. In Freeport, one casino is at Our Lucaya. The other is at the Isle of Capri Casino on Royal Palm Way. There is more information on gaming and casinos in the regional chapters.

Climate

The trade winds blow almost continuously here, creating a warm, agreeable climate that varies little throughout the year. September through May, when the temperature averages 70-

75°F, is the most refreshing time to visit. The rest of the year is somewhat warmer, with temperatures between 80° and 85°.

May is the rainy season.

Currency

Legal tender is the Bahamian dollar, which is always equivalent in value to the US dollar. Both US and Bahamian dollars are accepted interchangeably throughout the islands, and visitors are likely to receive change in mixed American and Bahamian currency.

Traveler's checks are accepted throughout the islands and may be cashed at banks and hotels. They will, however, add a service charge. Credit cards are widely accepted in Nassau and Freeport/Lucaya, and to a lesser extent on the Out Islands, where cash is still king. Be prepared to pay a service charge if you use American Express.

b British visitors should buy Bahamian dollars before traveling. The exchange rate often will be more favorable at home than in the Bahamas.

Dress

The dress code is casual and comfortable. Days are spent in shorts, swimsuits, slacks or jeans. Although the islands have been independent for more than 25 years, the influence of more than 250 years of British rule is still evident. You shouldn't wear swimsuits except at the pool or on the beach. Do not wear them in shops, restaurants, and on the streets of Nassau and Freeport/Lucaya.

In the evening, most people prefer to dress casual but smart – sport shirts and slacks. For more formal dining at some of the first-class restaurants and larger hotels, gentlemen should wear a tie and jacket; long skirts or cocktail dresses are preferred for ladies. On the Out Islands, except at some of the large resorts, dress is much more casual.

Electricity

All US and Canadian appliances can be used without adapters. Visitors from the United Kingdom will need adapters to 120 volts.

Ferries

Ah, this is the way to travel. Ferries in Nassau run between Prince George Dock and Paradise Island. On the Out Islands the ferry is often the only way of getting around. On Abaco, ferries run every hour or so between Treasure Cay, New Plymouth on Green Turtle Cay, and the Green Turtle Club (also on Green Turtle Cay), with various stops along the way. This round-trip takes about an hour to complete. From Marsh Harbour the ferry runs to Man-O-War Cay and back, and from Marsh Harbour to Hope Town on Elbow Cay and back. Once again, a round-trip takes about an hour. It's a lazy way to travel, but most enjoyable. There's nothing quite like a boat ride on a warm sunny day, especially when the scenery is spectacular and the sea the color of the palest jade. www.bahamasferries.com.

In Nassau and Freeport you will find at least a couple of cybercafés. There aren't many so it's a good idea to check exactly where they are before you go. You can check by going online at www.cybercafe.com.

In Nassau: The Cybercafé, PO Box N7442, Mall at Marathon, Nassau, Bahamas, Phone 242-394-6254, www.electrojack.com, anewton@electrojack.com. Open 8:30 am-8 pm. Cost: 15¢ per minute. There are six computers available, along with high-speed access for laptops.

In Freeport: The Cyberclub is quite a bit larger. PO Box F-40641, Seventeen Center, Grand Bahama, Phone 242-351-4560, www.grandbahama.net, cyberclub@grandbahama.net. Open Monday through Saturday, 9 am to 8 pm. Cost: $40 per month, but check for daily and weekly rates. 30 computers available plus high-speed access.

Most of the major hotels offer high-speed access via Ethernet cable. The cost runs from $12 to $20 per day, depending upon the hotel.

The IPass network offers dial-up service almost everywhere in the Bahamas and Turks & Caicos Islands. It's a bit of a pain to use – you have to get them to help you set up your computer for the Bahamas. To get a list of IPass providers, go to www.ipass.com and then click on "Individuals."

Select your country (Bahamas) and this is what you'll find:

"Worldwide Dialup - We are the solution for individuals, small to medium-size businesses and universities! Worldwide Dialup provides an easy to use, fully supported iPass dialup and broadband service, with 24x7x365 support, email with Spam and Virus Filtering, on-line account administration and a fully redundant network. Our staff provides technical assistance regardless of your operating system – from Windows to Mac to Palm, we can even point you in the right direction if you are using other non-supported systems for connectivity (Linux, Unix, etc). Our rates are extremely competitive!" They are based in Ada, Michigan and, yes, you'll have to call for current rates. Phone 616-682-4813, fax 616-682-1389.

Mail Boats

Even though the Out Islands are now almost all accessible by air, mail boats still ply the waters back and forth between the islands. The boats leave Nassau from Potter's Cay – located off East Bay Street under the east Paradise Island Bridge – about once a week, stopping at one or two of the Out Islands along the way. The journey takes about 12 hours, usually overnight. Schedules are somewhat random, subject to change and postponement. The mail boat is, however, an economical way to travel the islands, a lot of fun, and perhaps the most understated and unusual adventure available. The decks are crowded with Bahamians, freight, livestock and a variety of weird cargoes.

This is also a great way to make short trips to the Out Islands. For instance, the Bahamas Daybreak III leaves Nassau on Mondays at 7 pm, arrives at Governor's Harbour on Eleuthera at midnight, and returns to Nassau at 8 pm on Tuesday. You could spend the night at the Duck Inn or the Rainbow Inn, spend the next day sightseeing, swimming, snorkeling or whatever, then catch the boat and be back in your hotel by 1:30 am, just in time to get some sleep. Unfortunately, passage cannot be arranged in advance, but only after arrival in the Bahamas. For more information, call the dock master at Potter's Cay, Phone242-393-1064. You'll find detailed schedule and fare information within each regional chapter, and in the At a Glance section at the end of the book.

Visit www.bahamasgp.com.

Photography

The ocean wears a coat of many colors, ranging from the palest emerald green to the deepest indigo. The colors of the flowers – hibiscus, bougainvillea, goat's foot, and spider lily – seem a little brighter than anywhere else. The sand varies just a little from the palest pink to the tint of fine champagne. And then there's the clothing. Bahamians love bright colors. Light colored dresses, shirts, and hats set against rich brown skin offer rare opportunities for great photography. Gaily painted cottages, bustling streets alive with color, roadside fish markets, vast mangrove swamps, tiny harbors crowded with sailboats, lighthouses, and thousands of scenic bays, inlets, and beaches offer even more vistas for shutterbugs. If that's not enough, you can always dive into the underwater world where the colors are even brighter.

Here are some simple techniques to help you shoot better photos:

If you are shooting digital, take your laptop computer and a couple of extra memory chips. You'll also need a way to download your images – a card reader perhaps. If not a card reader, don't forget to take your camera's USB cable. If you can't take your computer, purchase a couple of 4GB chips and set your camera to shoot JPEG images at the "normal" or "medium" setting. This will allow you to shoot 1,000 images before you run out of memory. If you're using film, take more of it with you than you think you'll need, especially if you're shooting slides. Film is expensive locally and the type you prefer might not be available, especially in the Out Islands. Digital or film, you'll need extra batteries and a charger.

Digital photographers should set the ISO as low as possible – 100ISO is ideal. If you're shooting

35mm, use a low-speed film; 50 or 100ISO will produce the best results and less grain. The rule of thumb is: the lower the speed of the film, the sharper the image will be. In the interest of creating great pictures, use a low-speed film whenever you can, especially on bright sunny days. Use a high-speed film, or turn up the ISO on your digital camera, only with low light or when using a telephoto lens.

Shoot at the highest shutter speed you can. This will reduce camera shake. The longer the lens, the faster the shutter speed. You should never hand-hold a camera at a shutter speed slower than the focal length of the lens. For example you would only hand-hold a camera fitted with a 180mm lens when the shutter speed is set to 1/250 of a second or more; never slower. Likewise a 50mm lens could be hand-held with the shutter set to 1/60th of a second, but no slower.

Medical

The Bahamas are blessed with an excellent health service. Hospital facilities, public and private, are available in Nassau and Freeport. The Out Islands are served by health centers, clinics and general practitioner doctors. In an emergency, patients are flown to Nassau and treated at Princess Margaret Hospital.

You should be aware that most US medical insurance plans will not cover you while traveling abroad.

Most package operators offer travel protection insurance. This may cover some limited medical emergencies. Several insurance companies also offer cancellation insurance. They can be well worth the extra cost. Perhaps the best of these is CSA Travel Protection Insurance offered through travel agents and underwritten by Commercial Union Insurance Company. For more information, call your local travel agent or Phone 800-873-9855.

Visit www.csatravelprotection.com.

Insects are not much of problem, but take along some insect repellent just in case. And don't leave home without a good sunblock.

Rental Cars

If you have a valid US, Canadian or British driver's license, you can rent a car – even on the Out Islands, although what you get there might bring on a mild heart attack. Be sure to check the car's condition before you drive away.

Rates vary from around $60 to $90 per day, but are much cheaper if rented by the week. Special rates can be arranged through most agencies in advance of travel. In Nassau, the world-wide agencies – Avis (www.avis.com), Budget (www.budget.com), Dollar (www.dollar.com) and Hertz (www.hertz.com) – as well as several local companies, are found at the airport, hotels and several downtown locations. In Freeport, there's also an Avis office in the International Bazaar.

Remember, Bahamians drive on the left side of the road. It can at first be a little disconcerting, but you'll soon get used to it.

Shopping Hours

Although shops throughout the Bahamas are now permitted to open on Sundays and some national holidays, you'll find many remain closed. In Nassau, shops open daily from 9 am until 5 pm. In Freeport/Lucaya they open from 9 am until 8 pm, although many of the stores in the International Bazaar and at Port Lucaya stay open until 9 on Saturday evenings.

Taxis & Tours

In Nassau and Freeport/Lucaya, as well as most of the Out Islands, taxis are readily available. On the Out Islands, however, some taxis are showing their age. Almost always reliable, these taxis often offer a ride that can be an adventure all its own.

The Ministry of Tourism and the Bahamas Training College have established a number of specialty tour guide qualifications: ecotour guides, bird-watching guides, etc. On the Out Islands there are no tour buses and, as yet, few tour guides. This is where the taxi comes into its own. For as little as $16 an hour, your friendly driver will show you his island and tell you all about it. These drivers are experts on the history of their particular island, and are often able to tell the story in a form that's as entertaining as it is interesting.

Rates are often negotiable, especially if you are prepared to hire by the day. Meters are present in most cabs on the main islands, but they may not be activated. It's always best to negotiate a particular fare before embarking.

Taxis in Nassau and Freeport are always metered – make sure your driver turns his meter on – and can be found waiting for fares on busy downtown streets, and at the airports and hotels. Rates are generally reasonable. A ride from Nassau's airport to Paradise Island is about $20, and to Cable Beach about $15. In Freeport, the trip from the airport to the hotel district can cost anywhere from $8 to $12; the fare is the same from the hotel district to Pier One restaurant.

Tips are expected and a couple of dollars for a short trip will be enough. Taxis usually meet arriving flights and ferry boats, but it's advisable to make sure in advance. Speak with your hotel and have them arrange something for you if needed.

Telephones

When calling from the US, dial 242 and the local number. To call the US or Canada from the Bahamas, dial 1 + the area code and the local number.

Cell Phone s

Cell Phone use has gotten a lot easier over the last couple of years. Most manufacturers now build GSM (Global System for Mobiles) technology into their equipment as a matter of course, especially in Europe. In the US, all one needs is the properly-equipped cell phone , a call to your provider and a request for the international dialing option, and you're ready to go. The international dialing option will cost you nothing: the roaming service, however, can be quite expensive – anywhere from $1 to $5 per minute. If your Phone is not "international capable," you can always rent one from your local provider before you leave. It's not cheap – usually $40 to $50 per week – and then you'll also have to cough up for airtime, at least $1 per minute. Most of the national providers – Verizon, Cingular, etc. – offer cell Phone rental by the week. Other options in the USA include Roadpost (Phone 888-290-1606) and InTouch USA (Phone 800-872-7626). In the US, if you'd like to find out if your cell Phone will work in the Bahamas, call Phone 703-222-7161 or go online to

http://intouchglobal.com/travel.html.

Time

Time in the Bahamas coincides with that of the Eastern United States. If it's noon in Atlanta, it's noon throughout the Bahamas.

How to Use This Book

In the section on each individual island, you'll find everything you need to know to plan an enjoyable vacation. Travel planning tips, plus sections on sightseeing, shopping and the best beaches are offered. Then I focus on activities – from diving and hiking to bird-watching. The Out Islands are listed in alphabetical order after Grand Bahama and New Providence.

At the end of the book you'll find a section called At a Glance – a quick reference to all you need to know; no descriptions, just names and addresses listed by category.

Tourist Information

Information is readily available throughout the Bahamas. There are, for instance, two district offices of the Bahamas Ministry of Tourism on Eleuthera: one in Governor's Harbour, the other on Harbour Island. Ministry personnel are cheerful, ready and willing to help. Maps and brochures are free and yours for the asking.

Bahamas Ministry of Tourism, PO Box N-3701, Market Plaza, Bay Street, Nassau, Bahamas. Phone 242-322-7501; fax 242-328-0945.

The Grand Bahama Island Tourism Board, PO Box F-40251, Freeport, Grand Bahama Island. Phone 242-352-8365; fax 242-352-7849.

For information about the Out Islands, contact:

The Out Islands Promotion Board, 1100 Lee Wagener Boulevard, Suite 206, Ft. Lauderdale, Florida, 33315-3564. Phone 800-688-4752 (USA and Canada). In Ft. Lauderdale Phone 305-359-8099; fax 305-359-8098.

For brochures on the Bahamas, Phone 800-8BAHAMAS. You can also visit www.bahamasgo.com, where you'll find all sorts of useful information, some of which is not available anywhere else.

Bahamas Tourist Offices

150 East 52nd Street, New York, NY 10022. Phone212-758-2777; fax 212-753-6531.

One Turnberry Place, 19495 Biscayne Blvd., Suite 809, Aventura, FL 33180. ☐305-932-0051; fax 305-682-8758.

3450 Wilshire Blvd., Suite 1204, Los Angeles, CA 90010. Phone 213-385-0033; fax 213-383-3966.

8600 W. Bryn Mawr Avenue, Suite 820, Chicago, IL 60631. Phone 312-693-1500; fax 312-693-1114.

121 Bloor Street East, Suite 1101, Toronto, ON M4W 3M5, Canada. Phone416-968-2999; fax 416-968-6711.

3 The Billings, Walnut Tree Close, Guilford, Surrey, England, QV1 4VL. Phone01483-448990.

A Land of Adventure

In a nation completely surrounded by the clearest waters in the world, there are plenty of watersports. And while the great outdoors is where most people want to be, there's a lot to do here beyond the beach and the ocean. The shops and the nightlife of New Providence Island and Grand Bahama Island provide diversions that allow you to have a great vacation.

General information about what's available throughout the islands is listed in this section. More specific information about the attractions and activities on individual islands is given in each chapter, and the At a Glance section at the end of the book.

Bird Watching

Guides & Self-Guided Tours

With more than 25 inhabited islands and thousands of smaller rocks and cays, there is plenty of opportunity to explore different habitats and spot some rare birds. The three endemic species are the Bahama woodstar hummingbird, the Bahama swallow and Bahama yellowthroat warbler. Other prized birds include the white-tailed tropicbird, Bahama pintail, Bahama parrot, great lizard-cuckoo, loggerhead kingbird, Bahama mockingbird and the stripe-headed tanager, to name but a few. These birds cannot be found on all of the Bahamian Islands, so a birding guide can ensure you make the best use of your time.

Boating

Rentals

There are endless possibilities for getting out and about on the water – from the self-drive rental boat available by the hour, to the full-blown chartered day-sailor yacht that comes complete with captain and crew, not to mention champagne and lobster lunches. Most of the hotels have Hobe Cats, Sunfish or Sailfish for rent. Some even have Boston Whalers and other outboard-driven craft available. All come at a great variety of hourly or daily rates. Sometimes they are free. It's worth checking before you make your hotel reservations.

The islands have vast expanses of calm, clear open water, safe bays and inlets, and numerous convenient anchorages and marinas that offer everything from a quick lunch and a glass of cold beer to chilled champagne and a gourmet lobster dinner. All sizes of sailboats are available, with or without crew.

Arrangements can be made through any number of outlets, including your travel agent, hotel or one of the many special outfits you will find listed throughout the pages of this book.

Sea Kayaking & Sailing in the Exumas

If it's real adventure that you're looking for, consider a sea kayaking expedition in the Exumas. You can look forward to long hot days paddling the open waters between the islands of the chain, balmy nights under canvas, good food, and good company.

You have to be fairly fit to handle the often-strenuous exercise of paddling for hours at a time. But the sheer vastness of the seascapes, the pristine beaches, and the crystal waters make this a one-of-a-kind experience. See pages 231-34 for details on the various outfitters. Check pages 115-16 for Kayak Nature Tours.

Powerboat Adventures

Not for the faint-hearted, this is your chance to experience the thrills of off-shore powerboat racing in a certain degree of comfort, at least as much as one might be able to expect at speeds in excess of 50 miles per hour. Several companies offer this type of adventure, most of them operating out of Nassau. One offers day-trips to the Exumas – a truly excellent experience – and another has rides around Paradise Island. They'll take you anywhere in the Bahamas, provided you can afford the cost of a private charter. You'll find more detailed information in the chapters on Nassau and Paradise Island (page 74) and the Exumas (page 236).

Golf

Across the islands are a number of fine courses, some laid out by famous names in golf architecture: Robert Trent Jones Jr. and Sr., Pete Dye, Dick Wilson and Joe Lee, to name but a few.

The 13, Lucayan Golf Course

The Best Courses

The best courses are on the two most populated islands: New Providence and Grand Bahama. But the Out Islands, too, have some good courses. Most notable are those at the The Club on Eleuthera, The Treasure Cay Golf Club, Sandals Emerald Reef Golf Club on Great Exuma, and the small but challenging nine-hole course on Great Harbour Cay in the Berry Islands. All 18-hole courses on New Providence, Grand Bahama and the Out Islands have a complete range of facilities, including a resident pro, rental carts and clubs. Most facilities also offer clinics and private lessons.

Hiking & Bicycling

Opportunities to enjoy an afternoon, or even a week, hiking the quiet country lanes and beaches are just about endless. There's not a single island in the entire archipelago that doesn't offer some sort of hiking route.

Most hiking routes are lonely, often dusty, and without facilities. Be sure to carry everything you need, especially an adequate quantity of water and sun block.

Bicycling offers the opportunity to see the land at a more leisurely pace than by car or taxi. While bicycles are available for rent on the two main islands, they are not quite so easily come by in the Out Islands. Some of the hotels in the Out Islands offer them free of charge to their guests, and some do rent them to guests staying at other hotels. Check with your travel agent.

There are virtually no designated walking, hiking or bicycling trails on any of the islands. These activities are very much go-as-you-please affairs, especially on the Out Islands. The main roads are the first and most obvious choice, but there are also the beaches, of course, and hundreds of unmarked side roads that often end up at a secluded beach where you can enjoy a picnic lunch and a swim. At least in the Out Islands, there's no reason why you shouldn't wander at will. The locals are friendly and willing to give ideas, directions and the benefit of their knowledge about the best places to go and sites to see. Don't be afraid to ask.

Guided bike rides are offered by some of the larger hotels on New Providence Island, Pedal & Paddle Ecoventures in Nassau, Phone 242-362-2772, and Kayak Nature Tours on Grand Bahama Island, Phone 242-373-2485. Both offer guided rides and day-trips. Both use modern, off-road bikes.

If you are going to one of the more remote islands, consider taking your own bike. Check with the airline as to procedure and costs.

Honeymooning

The Bahamas epitomize romance. From the soft sounds of the steel drum and calypso wafting gently over the beaches on a warm evening under a spectacular sunset, to deserted beaches where the palms wave gently over an emerald sea, the islands have much to offer.

There are extensive opportunities for honeymooning, or even getting married, in the Bahamas. All major hotels and resorts on Grand Bahama and New Providence offer a full range of facilities, including everything from priest to cake. To get away from it all, consider honeymooning on one of the Out Islands – the Abacos, Eleuthera, or the Exumas. And for a really remote, even primitive, location, try Andros.

Here are some websites specializing in Bahamas weddings and honeymoons:

www.islanddreaming.com

www.weddinginthebahamas

www.coordinators.thebahamian.com

www.out-island-wedding.com

www.honeymoontravel.com

www.honemooncruiseshopper.com

www.wedding-world.com

Check first with your travel agent when making your booking and be sure to do so well in advance. The Bahamas are a very popular honeymoon destination and many suites are booked up a year or more in advance.

Horseback Riding

There's not much horseback riding on the islands and outfitters are often booked weeks in advance. There are stables on both Grand Bahama and New Providence. On New Providence, you can contact Happy Trails Stables, Phone 242-362-1820; on Grand Bahama, Pinetree Stables is at Phone 242-373-3600. The going rate is $40-$60 per hour, and you have a choice of English or Western saddles. Long rides along quiet country lanes lined with seagrapes, cocoa plums, casuarinas and white sandy beaches provide hours of quiet relaxation and often new friends and good company.

Parasailing

Parasailing is available from private operators at most of the major resorts both on New Providence Island and Grand Bahama Island.

Jet-Skiing

Jet-skiing is offered at most of the beachfront hotels on Grand Bahama and New Providence Islands, but not on the Out Islands because the skis damage the fragile coral heads. Rates vary from hotel to hotel, but start at around $40 for 30 minutes.

Shelling

Shelling is a hobby that can bring back memories of your vacation for years to come. Put on your swimsuit, leave the big cities behind, and go to the east end of Grand Bahama or New Providence at low tide. Wade out to the dark spots in the water where the seaweed grows. There, conch feed in the thousands. There's always someone around willing to clean the shells for you. Sand dollars are common, and literally hundreds of exquisite shells lie on the high water line of Out Island beaches.

Sport Fishing

For many Bahamians, fishing is not just a sport, it's the way they make their living. But sport fishing here is spectacular, and you don't have to be a world-class angler to take advantage of what the islands have to offer. In fact, it's okay if you've never fished before in your life. There are plenty of skilled guides willing to take you in hand and show you exactly how it's done. A couple of hours of instruction, a fast boat or a calm, shallow-water flat, and you're in business.

The Lure of Fishing

Nothing compares with the feeling you'll get aboard a slowly trolling boat on a calm sea under a hot summer sun, a heavy rod between your knees, and a can of something cold in your hand. And then it happens. There's a jerk on your line;

something's taken the bait, and in seconds you're involved in the fight of your life. But wait, the line goes slack, it's gone. No, it's still there, and suddenly the water a hundred yards from the boat explodes and the great fish is in the air. Your first sailfish hurls itself out of the water in a breathtaking arc. The sight leaves you speechless, awed and, for a moment, not knowing what to do next. And then it hits again and the fight is on. Slowly you reel in, the clutch slipping under the strain, three winds on the crank for every inch of line you gain. As suddenly as it began, it's over. Your opponent, exhausted at the side of the boat, is gaffed and hauled aboard. It's more than five feet long and weighs perhaps as much as 90 pounds – you won't know until you get it back to the scale on the dock, but it's a good one; you know it is. You go home at day's end satisfied and tired, but still excited, ready to do it all again tomorrow, the next day, next year.

There are many ways to fish in the Bahamas. Off-shore fishing is the premier choice, but there really is something for everyone and you don't need to charter an expensive deep-sea boat. You can do it from a small rental boat all by yourself, or even wade to your waist in the crystal waters of one of a hundred or more bonefish flats for a day of sport.

Other than the sailfish, the king of them all is perhaps the blue marlin. Catches of the big blue typically range from 100 to 300 pounds or more. Four and five hundred pounders are not uncommon and stories of the one that got away tell of fish in excess of 1,000 pounds. Fantasy? Perhaps; perhaps not.

Tuna is another fine blue-water catch. Every spring the bluefin make their annual run through the Bahamas, and anglers leave the docks in droves to participate in any one of a dozen or more tournaments from Bimini to Walker's Cay. Catches weigh from 100 to 800, even 900 pounds. There's also blackfin and yellowfin tuna – smaller, but no less fun to catch.

Other excellent deep-water species include the kingfish or king mackerel. They can be caught through the year, although peak time is during the spring and summer. Dolphin (the fish; not Flipper) are usually found fairly close in along the shoreline, weigh anywhere from five to 20 pounds, and are excellent to eat. Wahoo weigh 15 to 30 pounds; even 60 pounds is not unusual. They, too, make for good eating and are highly prized by sport fishermen. Wahoo are most often found lurking in the deep water off the edge of a reef. The amberjack is another prized sporting fish found most often during the summer months in the cooler, deep waters just off the edge of the reef and closer in-shore the rest of the year. Amberjack can run 20 to 40 pounds.

Sharks are common throughout the Bahamas, especially the Out Islands, and can be found in both shallow waters and deep. Bull sharks, blues, hammerheads, and tiger sharks abound. The truth is, however, that when one is caught, the fight usually lasts only as long as it takes for the shark's razor-like teeth to bite through the wire traces that hold him. Even so, you'll remember the battle for a long time to come.

The wily barracuda is found in large numbers, in shallow or deep waters. They can often be seen swimming close to the surface in the clear waters over reefs and sandy banks. Barracuda range in size from a few pounds to about 15 or 20 pounds and, small though they might be, you're sure of a good fight if you can get one on your hook.

Unfortunately, barracuda are often the victims of ciguatera poisoning and are, therefore, risky to eat.

For good eating, you can't beat grouper. Grouper – black, Nassau and yellowfin – can be found swimming lazily around, close to the bottom on the reefs throughout the Bahamas. Catches ranging from 15 to 25 pounds are the norm, and fish of 30 to 45 pounds are not uncommon. Often, your hotel will be willing to clean and cook grouper for you. There's nothing quite like a grouper steak, caught in the afternoon and eaten the same evening. The snapper too, may be caught on reefs throughout the islands. Most common are the red and gray variety and, though a fish may weigh only a pound or two, fresh-caught snapper is delicious.

Bonefishing

Inside the reef, before you reach the deep waters of the ocean where glamorous, deep-water sportfish hog the limelight, there's a second, very exciting sporting opportunity – bonefishing. The elusive bonefish, often called the ghost fish, is rapidly becoming one of the most popular sportfish on the islands. Until quite recently, bonefishing was almost unheard of among mainland anglers. Today, people from around the world flock here in search of this hard-fighting denizen of the flats.

Bonefish, so named for the huge numbers of bones in their bodies, live in deep water and come up onto the flats to feed. That's where you'll have to go to find them. Unlike most deep-water sportfish, they offer not only a good fight, but the thrill of a hunt as well.

Bonefish, like deer, must be stalked, and they are just as skittish. Make a wrong move at the wrong time and your quarry will be gone in a flash, leaving you standing alone in the water, totally frustrated, and wondering what went wrong.

Bonefish are not very big. They weigh in around six to 15 pounds, with some growing as large as 20 pounds.

You'll need a guide who knows the area and where the best flats are found. Many hotels offer bonefishing packages that include the services of a reliable and experienced guide. If not, don't be afraid to ask. The hotel desk is the best place to start, but many taxi drivers know just who to put you in touch with. Most boat rental companies and dive companies will also know of someone.

Bonefishing is good almost everywhere in the islands, from Abaco to the Acklins, and from Bimini to Eleuthera. Unlike most other sportfishing, it is good throughout the year. There are a number of ways to go about it. It's claimed that in some areas bonefish can be caught from the dock, or by casting into the surf, or from a skiff. But the best way is to hunt them down on foot on the lonely flats of the Out Islands. This is where your guide will earn his fee. He will know where to go, what bait to use – fly or jig – and he'll guide you through the basics of how to fish for the ghost.

Bonefish come up onto the flats in schools and can be seen first in the near distance as a dark stain in the crystal-clear water above the white sandy bottom, then as a vast, surging ripple on the surface of the water as maybe a hundred fish move like a flock of birds, this way and that, across the flats, tails cleaving the water. Then you see them, shadowy gray streaks flashing over the white sand, ghostly, moving fast.

To hunt bonefish, move slowly, disturbing the water as little as possible. Keep your eyes on the school, not on the sandy bottom beneath your feet. Take one step at a time, until you're close enough to try a cast. Aim tour fly or jig close to the center of the school. If you're lucky, there's a slight tug, then a stronger one, and the surface of the water explodes in a frenzy of white water and struggling fish; and he's off like a runaway horse leaving you hanging on to your rod, reel screaming, spinning, as 150 yards of line disappears seaward in what seems less than a second. Then he turns, heads in another direction as you wind in frantically to take up the slack, beginning to reel him in, fighting every inch of the way.

Bonefishing guides cost about $250 for a full day, or $150 for a half-day. Bring food and beverage. If you don't have your own gear, your guide can supply everything you need.

If you've never bonefished before, the best way is to purchase one of the packages offered by many of the islands' hotels. These require only that you bring yourself and a willingness to do as you're told. You can expect to spend anywhere from $350 for a three-night stay, to more than $2,000 for seven nights in a luxury accommodation (see individual chapters for specific details).

Tournaments

There's a year-round series of competitive fishing events designed to make things as interesting as possible for all participants, novice and veteran alike. The best-known and most popular is the Bahamas Billfish Championship Tournament, held during the spring and early summer each year at five different locations.

Anglers are welcome to take part in all or as many legs as they wish. The first two legs are held in April at Bimini and Walker's Cay. In May, the tournament moves to Treasure Cay and Boat Harbour, and then ends at Chub Cay in June. For details and registration, Phone 305-923-8022.

The Bimini Big Game Club sponsors a number of tournaments. These include the mid-winter Wahoo Tournament in February, the Annual Bacardi Rum Billfish Tournament in March, the Bimini Festival in May, the Family Tournament in August, the Small B.O.A.T. Tournament for boats under 27 feet in September, and another Wahoo Tournament in November. The Bimini International Light Tackle Bonefish Tournament consists of two legs – one in January, the other in February. Phone 800-327-4149 for more information and reservations.

The Penny Turtle Billfish Tournament is held at the Great Abaco Beach Resort each May; Phone 800-468-4799. The Billfish Foundation's Tag Tournament is held in May at the Walker's Cay Hotel and Marina on Abaco; Phone 800-WALKERS. The Green Turtle Cay Yacht Club hosts a fishing tournament in May; Phone 242-365-4271. The What's Out There Tournament is held at Great Harbour Cay in April; Phone 800-343-7256. The Boat Harbour Billfish Championship is held at the Marsh Harbour Resort in Abaco in June; Phone 305-920-7877.

The Bahamas Bonefish Annual Bash is held in February at the Club Peace and Plenty on Exuma; Phone 800-525-2210. The Andros Big Yard Bonefishing and Bottom Fishing Tournament is held in June; call the Bahamas Tourism Office at Phone 800-32-SPORT. There's also a bonefishing tournament held in mid-July at the Staniel Cay and Yacht Club on Exuma; Phone 242-355-2011. Bonefishing, as well as big game fishing, is a part of the Bahamian Outer Islands International Gamefish Tournament held in March; Phone 800-426-0466 for location, details and registration.

For a full listing and schedules, contact the Bahamas Tourism Office, Phone800-32-SPORT, or the Bahama Out Islands Promotion Board at Phone 800-688-4725.

Fishing Licenses & Permits

There are no restricted fishing seasons; it's open season throughout the year on whatever you want to catch. Licenses are not required if you're fishing from a Bahamian-registered boat. You will, however, need to obtain a sport-fishing permit if using your own craft. A single-visit permit costs $20 and is available at your legal port of entry into the Bahamas. An annual permit will cost you $250. You can also obtain your permit in advance by contacting the Department of Fisheries, PO Box N-3028, Nassau, Bahamas, Phone242-393-1777.

Only hook and line fishing is allowed in the Bahamas; use of a speargun is illegal. In fact, spearguns themselves are illegal in the Bahamas.

The number of lines per boat is limited to six in the water at any one time.

The bag limit per person per boat for dolphin, kingfish and wahoo, or any combination of the three species, is six. Above that limit, fish should be released unharmed, as should all fish unless they are to be used for food.

Planning your fishing trip is easy. Many hotels offer packages of between three and eight days, with everything you need included in the rate: boat, bait, box lunches and gear. In some cases, even the use of a small sailboat is included (see specific chapters for package details).

Marine National Parks

More and more, the government of the Bahamas is concerned with protecting the fragile ecosystem and expanding the national park system, especially marine parks. At the time of writing, these included:

Peterson Cay National Park of Grand Bahama, a 1½-acre cay and its surrounding reef system.

Black Sound Cay National Reserve on Green Turtle Cay, Abaco, a two-acre mangrove reserve.

Tilloo Cay National Reserve, Abaco, 11 acres of exposed shoreline.

Pelican Cays Land Sea Park, Cherokee Sound, Great Abaco, a 2,100-acre undersea park with an extensive system of caves and reefs.

Exuma Cays Land & Sea Park, more than 112,640 acres of land and sea marine reserve of outstanding natural beauty.

Conception Island National Park, a 2,100-acre island bird and turtle sanctuary.

Union Creek Reserve, Great Inagua, a 4,940-acre enclosed reserve incorporating a tidal creek.

While you are welcome to visit these parks and reserves, preferably with a guide, it is an offense to remove anything from the parks, alive or dead. This includes seashells.

Sightseeing

Local operators on Grand Bahama and New Providence offer a wide variety of sightseeing tours. Many taxi drivers also psrovide specialized sightseeing tours and will often know more about the sights and sounds of the islands than the scheduled tour operators. In Nassau, one such driver who comes readily to mind is Mr. Pemmi Sutherland. The man is an absolute mine of information and trivia, and a great source of fun in the bargain. Pemmi can be reached through Li'l Murph Taxis, Phone242-325-3725.

On the Out Islands, sightseeing tours are provided by local taxi drivers, who can be hired by the hour, but come much cheaper if contracted for the full day.

Snorkeling & Diving

Scuba Diving

Diving off the Bahamas is excellent. Dive operators on most of the islands can take you on scheduled dives, or to locations of your own choosing.

For the most part, the waters off the Bahamas are very clear, shallow and offer an abundance of coral reefs and gardens for you to explore, as well as shipwrecks, modern and ancient.

Unless you are an experienced diver, it's probably best to work with an operator, especially if you want to go wreck or shark diving.

Dive Sites

The dive sites listed throughout this book are, for the most part, remote and difficult to get to without a qualified guide. The locations of most listed sites in the Out Islands are not marked in any way – on maps or in the ocean – and are the closely guarded secrets of the local dive operators who make their living taking divers out on guided tours. If you want to see a particular site, ask your operator. If there are enough people interested in the site to make a full boat, it will cost no more than the regular half-day or full-day tour. If not, you'll have to rent the boat and guide on your own, which can be expensive.

a It is not recommended that you go off on your own. Local knowledge of the waters and currents is essential, and it's dangerous to dive without such knowledge, especially where shipwrecks are concerned.

Snorkeling

Snorkeling can be enjoyed almost anywhere with clear waters. The only place you need permission to swim is off private beaches.

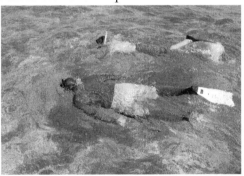

You should seek professional advice before taking off into the deep. It matters little where you might be staying; even on the most remote of the Out Islands there will always be someone available to warn you about the currents or other dangers at any given spot.

Dangers

Sharks, predators of the deep, have gained an undeserved reputation. But sharks kill only when hungry. Shark attacks are extremely rare, especially in the Bahamas. They say you have more of a chance of being twice-struck by lightning than of being attacked by a shark.

Moray eels, on the whole, are nocturnal creatures and like to be left alone inside their chosen lair. There are a few that might have become accustomed to humans – and the handouts they have come to expect from them – but those that haven't can, if disturbed or threatened, give you a very nasty bite. Stay at a respectful distance.

Barracuda are not really dangerous, just scary-looking, especially with their rather frightening and ever-present grin. The sleek, silver tiger of the ocean is a curious creature, however, and will often follow you around, which can be a little unnerving. If you happen to be feeding the local reef fish, which you shouldn't do, you should always be on the lookout for something bigger. A barracuda after his share of the pie will attack like lightning and, although he's only after your hand-out, it might be your hand he takes.

Reef fish tend to be curious. They're not dangerous, but you might find them nipping at your fingers, toes and hair.

Rays, on the whole, are not dangerous. Tread on a stingray buried in the sand, however, and you're probably in for a trip to the local hospital. The ray's first reaction is self-preservation, and its natural instinct is to lash out with its murderous tail. Unless threatened or trodden on, however, it's pretty much harmless and fascinating to watch as it flaps over the sandy bottom. Just be careful where you're putting your feet.

Scorpionfish lie in wait for the unwary on coral heads or close to the ocean floor. They have a set of thick spines on their backs that can inflict a nasty sting. Keep your hands clear.

The stonefish, often hard to see due to its camouflage, can also give you a nasty sting. Look carefully before you touch anything.

Jellyfish, transparent and often difficult to see, are almost all harmless. There are, however, some that are not. It's best to avoid them all.

Coral is often sharp, and tiny pieces can become dislodged in cuts and abrasions. If this should happen, you'll be in for a painful couple of days. Fire coral should not be handled at all. Your best bet is not to touch any coral – not only because it can hurt you, but also because it's a delicate, living organism.

Sea urchins are spiky little black or red balls that lie on the sandy ocean floor or in nooks and crannies among coral heads in the shallow waters of the reef. Step on a sea urchin with bare feet at your peril. The spines are brittle, often barbed, and will give you a very nasty experience. Fortunately, urchins are easily seen and thus easily avoided. Keep a sharp lookout and don't touch.

b If you do happen to get stung by coral, jellyfish, or an urchin, you can treat the sting first with vinegar. This will neutralize the poison. Then you should get some help from the local drugstore to ease the pain.

Wreck Diving

It is said that there are more than 500 shipwrecks in the Bahamas, and it's probably true. Some of these wrecks, especially those that allow access to their interiors, can be dangerous and even experienced divers should not go into them alone. There are plenty of guides and dive operators who do know their way around. Many wrecks are infested with fire coral. Many more are home to moray eels that are not dangerous if you give them space.

SAFETY

Take reasonable precautions and stay alert. You'll get into trouble only if you do something you shouldn't, are neglectful, or fail to take note of expert advice. Never dive alone.

Sun Seeking

There are literally thousands of beaches here – some crowded, some so deserted you won't see another human being for weeks at a time. Great expanses of sugar-white sand and the palest of green waters stretch for mile after sun-soaked mile. On New Providence and Grand Bahama, almost every hotel is either on or close to a beach. Those that aren't provide free shuttle services back and forth to a carefully selected and monitored beach.

The Out Islands boast of some of the finest beaches in the world, including Fernandez Bay on Cat Island, Harbour Island off Eleuthera, Rolleville on Great Exuma, Great Harbour Cay on the Berry Islands, Staniard Creek on Andros, Stocking Island off George Town on Great Exuma, and the entire shoreline of Mayaguana Cay just east of Acklins Island.

Tennis

Many of the larger and resort hotels have excellent tennis facilities. The largest is the 20-court tennis complex at Club Med on Paradise Island (see page 50). There are also fine facilities at other hotels on Paradise Island, Cable Beach, on Grand Bahama at Freeport/Lucaya, and on Eleuthera.

Water Skiing

The best sites for water skiing are off Paradise Island and Cable Beach in Nassau, and off the beaches at Freeport/Lucaya. Many of the big hotels on the two main islands of New Providence (Nassau) and Grand Bahama offer water skiing, as do some of the larger hotels and resorts on the Out Islands.

Windsurfing

Warm trade winds blow almost constantly, providing never-ending opportunities. Equipment can be rented quite easily on New Providence and Grand Bahama, and some of the largest hotels and resorts offer windsurfing free of charge. On the Out Islands, however, windsurfing gear is harder to find.

Nightlife

Nassau and Freeport/Lucaya, with four casinos and a number of nightclubs and theaters between them, are the hot-spots for nightlife and entertainment. To experience the warm summer evenings, the colorful dress of the Bahamians, and the lilting sounds of West Indian steel drums and calypso music, is to capture some of the real feeling of the islands.

Shopping

The Bahamas have shopping with a difference. The prices are not always what you might hope for, but searching for a bargain is half the fun. From the tiny street market in George Town on Great Exuma to the International Marketplace in Freeport to the world-famous Straw Market on Bay Street in Nassau, there are thousands of opportunities to browse, argue and bargain. Haggling over price can be a fun experience.

January: New Years' Day (Jan 1) is a public holiday.

April: Good Friday (1st Friday in April) and Easter Monday (Monday following Easter) are public holidays.

May: Whit-Monday. This public holiday follows Whitsunday (also known as Pentecost), the seventh Sunday after Easter.

June: Labor Day (June 1) is a public holiday.

July: Independence Day (July 10) is a public holiday that celebrates the Bahamas' independence from Britain. Parades and fireworks.

August: Emancipation Day, the first Monday in August, commemorates the end of slavery in the Bahamas in 1834.

September: Annual Bahamas Jazz Festival – an international event held the first week in September.

October: Discovery Day (Oct 12) is a public holiday celebrating Christopher Columbus' first landing in the Bahamas.

November: Guy Fawkes Festival (Nov 10) is celebrated on Eleuthera in honor of the capture of Guy Fawkes, who attempted to blow up the Houses of Parliament in England in 1605.

Central Banks Art Exhibition and Competition (Nov 16) is a national competition for artists under

26 years old, who showcase their works in a variety of media.

December: Christmas Day is a public holiday.

Boxing Day/Junkanoo Parade (Dec 26): The biggest public celebration on the islands, especially in Nassau. This is a traditional British holiday, when the wealthy boxed their Christmas dinner leftovers and presented them to their servants.

By Air

Several major airlines provide scheduled service into Freeport. Of these, **American Airlines** (Phone 800-433-7300, www.aa.com) offers the most options, although everything must connect through Miami.

By Cruise Ship

Five major cruise lines offer three- and four-night, regularly scheduled cruises to the Bahamas. Royal Caribbean International operates the Sovereign of the Seas out of Miami. The ship does its three-night itinerary leaving port on Fridays for Nassau and their private island of Coco Cay. The four-night cruise leaves port on Mondays, and it too visits Nassau and Coco Cay. Rates start at around $350 per person, depending upon the season. Phone 800-453-4022. www.royalcaribbean.com.

Carnival Cruise Lines operates ships out of Miami and Port Canaveral on three- and four-night itineraries. The Ecstasy leaves Miami on Fridays for the three-night cruise. The Fantasy leaves Port Canaveral for three nights on Thursdays, and on Sundays for four nights. Rates start at around $350 per person, depending on the season. Phone 888-CARNIVAL. www.carnival.com.

Celebrity Cruise lines sail out of Fort Lauderdale to the Bahamas. Phone 800-647-2251 or http://www.celebritycruises.com.

Norwegian Cruise Lines sail to the Bahamas from New York City. Phone 877-857-3513 or www.**norwegian-cruises**-vacations.com.

Disney's cruise ships sail out of Port Canaveral on three- and four-night itineraries, and is the most expensive option. The three- and four-night cruise itineraries, usually combined with a three- or four-day visit to Walt Disney World, include a stop in Nassau and a visit to Disney's private island, Castaway Cay. Rates start at $450 per person for the three-night cruise and $530 for the four-night option; these rates are for the cruise only and do not include the Disney World option. Phone 800-511-1333. www.disneycruise.com.

Package Vacations

Package options to Freeport and Grand Bahama are not as readily available as those to Nassau and New Providence. Several independent operators offer packages to one or two designated hotels. Other than that you'll need a creative travel agent's help to build your own package.

A number of tour operators provide air/hotel packages. **Delta Dream Vacations**, **American FlyAAWay Vacations**, **Vacation Express**, **Travel Impressions**, and **Apple Vacations** all offer packages to Nassau. American FlyAAWay Vacations, **Princess Vacations**, Travel

Impressions, Vacation Express and Apple also offer packages to Grand Bahama.

Package vacations are usually arranged by a travel agent and will typically include airfare from a major US or European gateway, round-trip airport/hotel transfers, accommodations at a hotel chosen from the package operator's inventory, and hotel taxes. Another option is an "all-inclusive" package. This will include, not only your round-trip airfare, airport/hotel transfers, and accommodations, but all of your meals and drinks (alcoholic and soft), gratuities, golf and watersports.

Is an all-inclusive package worth the extra cost? In general, yes; especially when you consider the cost of beverages: even the non-alcoholic versions of the exotic drinks will cost $5 to $6, and soft drinks are $2 to $3.

Hotels in most packages range from Tourist Class to Superior Deluxe, and are supposed to be inspected by the tour operator on a regular basis; some do, indeed, carry out such inspections. Remember, however, that you are not dealing with the same standards as in the United States, Canada or England (see the definitions under *Accommodations* on pages 17-18). I recommend that you NOT book a package with a hotel rated less than "Deluxe."

Getting Around

In a city the size of Freeport, getting around is not difficult. Everywhere, taxi drivers await. They know the best places to go for entertainment, where the best beaches are, and more about the local history and traditions than most of the accredited guides. Rental cars, mopeds and bicycles are always available from a number of international and local agencies. You can also choose from a number of guided trips and tours to the many attractions around the harbor, under the sea, and into the outback.

The main roads are mostly good, especially around Freeport/Lucaya.

B Remember to drive on the left side of the road and, when crossing the road, look to the right.

By Bicycle

Bicyclists will be pleased to learn that the terrain is mostly flat. Many attractive locations are within easy pedaling distance of Freeport and Lucaya. You might want to give **Taino Beach** a try. It's less than three miles from the hotel district of Lucayan Beach and well worth the effort. Take Seahorse Road from Lucaya to Midshipman Road and turn right. Cycle about a mile and turn right again onto West Beach Road. Turn right at the Stoned Crab sign and follow the road down to Taino Beach, where you'll find a long stretch of sugar-white sand dotted with umbrellas.

By Car

Suggested Trips

The settlement of **West End** is a leisurely 45 minutes away from Freeport. Take the West Sunrise Highway and the Queen's Highway along the well-paved road to the oldest settlement on Grand Bahama. You'll find a number of other small towns and villages along the way, each with unique attractions.

If you decide to go east, you'll need to set aside the entire day. The two- to three-hour drive will take you through a number of odd little settlements. Take the East Sunrise Highway from Lucaya, past Fortune Beach and on to **Gold Rock Beach**, a part of the Lucayan National Park, where you can enjoy caves and mangrove swamps and feed fish and ducks. From Gold Rock Beach, continue on through Bevan's Town to **High Rock**, where you can enjoy the scenery. Then it's on to **Pelican's Point, McClean's Town**, and perhaps a boat ride out to **Sweeting's Cay**, a tiny settlement right at the end of Grand Bahama. Electricity did not come to this quaint little community until 1994 and, from all accounts, it generated quite a celebration. The locals turned out in force to see the first light turned on. It's a long way to McClean's Town, but the trip is well worth the effort.

Car Rental Companies

- **Avis**: Phone 242-352-7666, 800-331-2112, www.avis.com. $65 and up per day, plus $12 per day insurance. **Courtesy**: Phone 242-352-5212. $69 and up per day; insurance is included.

- **Econo Car & Motor Bike Rental**: □242-351-6700. $55 and up per day, including insurance.

- **Hertz**: Phone 242-352-9250, 800-654-3001, www.hertz.com. $60 and up per day, plus $12 per day insurance.

- **Dollar**: Phone 242-352-9325, 800-800-3665, www.dollar.com. $50 and up per day, plus $10 per day insurance.

- **Sears Rent-A-Car**: Phone 242-352-5953. $55 and up per day, plus $10.50 per day insurance.

Shopping

You'll find a world of goodies, trinkets, jewelry, perfume, and gifts, and almost everything at bargain prices – taxable goods, that is. Grand Bahama's duty-free status makes it a mecca for those with money to spend and the time to shop around.

Grand Bahama has taken advantage of its unique status and, far from being a center for cheap and shoddy goods, you'll find it *the* place for brand names at good prices.

Of course, alcohol and perfumes have always been at the top of most lists to take home. Top-of-the-line imported brands available duty-free save around 40% off list prices in the United States, and even more if you are from the UK.

Beyond bargain drinks and fragrances, there are many other dutiable products you might want to buy: luxurious crystal and china, fine jewelry, leather goods, silver, gold, emeralds, all sorts of electrical goods and electronic gadgets; even cashmere and pure woolen goods.

The rainbow ends when you reach Customs on your return home. Make sure you know exactly what your duty-free allowance is; if you exceed it, you'll have to pay.

Of all that's available to shoppers on Grand Bahama, and there is an awful lot, most of it is sold at the International Bazaar and the Port Lucaya Marketplace.

The International Bazaar

Next to the Royal Oasis Golf Resort & Casino, this is a vast complex of shops, stores, boutiques, restaurants, cafés and interesting little diversions. You can spend hours perusing the diversity of goods and sampling the food. www.grand-bahama.com/bazaar.htm. Open Mon-Sat, 9:30/10 am-6 pm; some stores open Sun 10 am-5 pm.

Be sure to check out the **Bahamian Souvenir Outlet** in the Indian section of the Bazaar. This is a one-stop shop for gifts and souvenirs. Some are made locally. The list includes Bahamian perfumes, music, books, shell jewelry, Anna Karina Bahamian coin jewelry, sea life jewelry, coconut shell figurines, clocks, and straw products.

For liquor, head to the **Burns House**. They carry just about every international brand you can think of, plus the local stuff. **Butler & Sands** is the place to go for fine wines.

For resort wear, cruise wear, and other casual clothing, **Bye-Bye Bahamas** is the hottest new outlet on the island.

To find something very special, visit to **Colombian Emeralds International.**

Fragrance of the Bahamas offers a complimentary tour of the working perfume factory. **Parfum de Paris** is in the heart of the French section of the Bazaar, but there are many more options.

The Port Lucaya Marketplace

Just across the way from the Atlantik Beach Hotel, this is a vast complex of shopping and dining opportunities, with all sorts of duty-free outlets. One that's not to missed is the **Golden Nuggets** store, which offers terrific buys on close-out jewelry, a vast selection of gold chains, bracelets, bangles and precious and semi-precious gemstone jewelry at prices that are hard to believe.

Linens of Lucaya has a selection of quality linens and exotic gifts – all at savings of up to 50% from prices of similar goods in the United States.

Pusser's is the place to go for lunch or dinner. This very British pub, restaurant and boutique offers great food and drink, as well as upscale clothing, including slacks and shirts.

Sightseeing

Grand Bahama is crammed with attractions and light adventures. Those described here are some of the most worthwhile.

Garden of the Groves

At the intersection of Midshipmen Road and Magellan Drive, this 12-acre botanical garden (Phone 242-373-5668) is dedicated to the memory of Freeport's founders, Wallace and Georgette Groves. It's acknowledged as one of the finest botanical centers in the Caribbean, a floral and water paradise of hibiscus, bougainvillea, powder puff, chenille, screw pines and Washington palms. A walk through the garden will take you through tiny floral communities, including the Citrus Grove, Fern Gully and Bougainvillea Walk. Along the way, keep an eye out for curly tailed lizards and wander beneath ornamental waterfalls. Take a rest in the tiny Chapel on the Hill, visit the Cactus Garden and the Hanging Gardens, and pause to look at a replica of Freeport's first airport terminal building, a tiny wooden hut with barely enough room for two people. The walk through Fern Gully will take you 20 feet below the surrounding gardens to a 400-foot pathway lined with exotic plants and flowers, heady with the sweet smells of the island's year-long summer. Guided tours available. Petting zoo. Wedding ceremonies offered. Open daily from 10 am to 4 pm. $10 for adults; $7 for kids. www.gardenofthegroves.com.

Lucayan National Park

This park is 20 miles east of Lucaya on the East Sunrise Highway and is easily accessible by taxi, tour bus, moped, auto, or public bus (take the bus to High Rock and make arrangements with the driver to drop you off and pick you up). Admission is $3 and the park is open daily from 9 am to 4 pm. The park can be reached at Phone 242-352-5438. www.grand-bahama.com/lucayan.htm.

The park is the result of efforts by the Bahamas National Trust, with some help from Operation Raleigh.

Operation Raleigh

This is an international group of young people who travel by boat – in the tradition of their namesake, Sir Walter Raleigh – and lend a hand with various scientific projects. They laid most of the trails and boardwalks throughout the Lucayan National Park.

In addition to its wealth of flora and fauna, the 40-acre park has a number of special and interesting features. Extending on both sides of the highway, it features a long, looping walk and a series of caves to the north, with a large mangrove swamp and deserted beach area to the south.

The parking lot is on the north side of the road. From there, follow the path to **Ben's Cave**, the first of two caves, named for Ben Rose, the diver and biologist who discovered it. Ben's Cave is part of an underground, underwater system of caverns said to be among the largest of its kind in the world. The cave is also home to the tiny remipedia (oar foot), a crustacean found nowhere else in the world. A little further on along the trail you'll see another opening. This is the **Burial Mound Cave**, where, in 1986, archaeologists found four skeletons on the floor, along with evidence of pre-Columbian settlement. The skeletons were the remains of a group of local Lucayan Indians.

On the south side of the road a narrow trail takes you across a large expanse of mangrove swamp and a section of **Gold Rock Creek** to the ocean and Gold Rock Beach. Be sure to take your swimming gear along. For most of the walk you'll hike across a vast watery area via a series of narrow boardwalks. Along the way, you'll see a wide assortment of plants and wildlife. The trail will take you past strange-looking, bonsai-like ming trees and, if the season is right, a variety of colorful orchids.

In the saltwater creek you may see a lurking barracuda and other saltwater fish, including gray snapper. There's also a covey of small wild ducks, all quacking and flapping, busily pursuing their daily lives in the swamp.

Beyond the mangrove swamp lies one of the highest coastal dunes on the island, a richly vegetated area of cocoplum, casuarina, seagrape, cinnecord, and other species of tropical trees.

At the far end of the trail, **Gold Rock Beach** lies on the windswept south side of the island. It's often deserted, but always appealing, with magnificent views of the wide sandy shore, emerald waters, and Gold Rock itself jutting up out of the ocean a half-mile offshore. Gold Rock Beach is one of those places you see in commercials. It's a strip of tropical paradise where, in all likelihood, you'll find yourself alone to swim and snorkel in the clear shallow waters.

Return to your vehicle by continuing on along the trail, which loops around the park, over the mangroves, to end at the park entrance where it began.

Rand Memorial Nature Center

On Settler's Way, just two miles from Freeport and three miles from Lucaya, this is a 100-acre nature reserve where you can spend an interesting hour or two learning about Grand Bahama's flora and fauna. If you enjoy bird watching, this is the place for you. More than 40 species of birds, including turkey vultures, hairy woodpeckers, Bahama yellowthroats, indigo buntings, American redstarts, Greater Antillean pewees, and American red-tailed hawks, inhabit the park.

Take a **guided tour** of the facility, the only way to see and really understand its scope, and you'll be introduced to many of the smaller birds as they fly in for a tidbit casually tossed into the air by your guide; it's very entertaining. The tour will take you on a pleasant walk along the 2,000-foot nature trail that meanders back and forth among the flowering plants, orchids, poinsettias, periwinkles, hibiscus, impatiens, morning glories and more, to a freshwater pond at the end. There, a flock of West Indian flamingos will rush to meet you, ready for their treat – a morsel of dog food, which they'll devour with great relish. You may also see butterflies, blue-tailed lizards, tree frogs and curly tailed lizards.

Traditional Lucayan Village

A replica of a Lucayan village includes small *canayes*, round family dwellings, thatched with palm leaves. The chieftain's house is square, reflecting his all-powerful image, while the *cacique bohio*, a place of worship, is hexagonal.

The nature center is open Monday through Friday from 9 am until 4 pm. Guided tours of the sanctuary are conducted daily at 10 am and 2 pm. If you want to do the tour alone, you can. Admission is $5 for adults and $3 for children five-12; free for children under five. Phone 242-352-5438.

Ask for a bird checklist to help you recognize those you see.

Seaworld Explorer

Seaworld Explorer (Phone 242-373-7863), owned by Superior Watersports of Freeport, is one of the best ways to explore the undersea world and certainly the most reasonably priced. The *Explorer* is half-sightseeing cruiser and half-submarine. The neat thing about it is that you'll have the excitement of the submarine experience without ever being submerged.

The cruise costs just $39 per person. It begins with a ride, topside, of about a mile out to the reef, where you'll descend the stairs to the observation deck. This is where things get really interesting. The lower deck is a narrow chamber with seats for up to 30 people. The large undersea windows are angled so that you can look downward as well as outward, a definite advantage over the *Atlantis*-type submarine in Nassau. For the next hour you'll move slowly over the coral reef, observing all sorts of coral formations and a multitude of gaily colored marine life.

Be sure to take along your camera and some high-speed film. You may see sharks, spotted eagle rays, stingrays or barracuda, and you'll certainly see parrotfish, sergeant majors, triggers, queen angels, puffers, and a lot more. The *Seaworld Explorer* excursion is one of the best values on the island.

The Dolphin Experience

The Dolphin Experience (Phone 800-992-DIVE, 242-373-1244, info@unexso.com, www.unexso.com), on the dock in Freeport in the same building as, and owned by, UNEXSO, also offers a unique encounter. It's a fascinating and often soul-stirring experience where you'll meet, close-up, one of nature's most lovable and intelligent creatures: the Atlantic bottlenose dolphin. Be sure to wear clothes that you don't mind getting wet.

Your experience – actually, there are a couple of different programs – starts at UNEXSO's headquarters on the dock across from Our Lucaya.

You'll board a boat for a 20-minute ride out to Sanctuary Bay where the dolphins live.

UNEXSO is an acronym for the organization's full title: The UNderwater EXplorer's SOciety.

The first things you'll see when you arrive at the facility are the tops of the huge pens that keep the dolphins separated from each other and safe from marauding sharks. Then, you'll take the boardwalk over the water and the dolphin pens to the observation platform, where you'll actually meet the animals.

Close Encounter

The Dolphin Close Encounter program allows you meet the dolphins face-to-face; well, bottlenose-to-face. Before you do, however, you'll listen to a 15-minute talk that dispels the myths and legends that have built up around this finny creature. While the talk is being given, a couple of your soon-to-be playmates are carousing about the pool near where you're sitting.

Dolphins are not quite the close cousins you've been led to believe, and they don't have supernatural healing powers either. It's true that they are extremely intelligent and love to play, as you'll soon find out.

When the talk is ended, your instructor will call you into the water – it's not deep – where you'll stand in pairs facing each other. The two dolphins then swim into the gap between you and your partner, and you'll be allowed to stroke, pet and rub them down; they love it. You'll be surprised, too, at the size of these creatures. They are some eight to 12 feet long and can weigh in at 500-700 pounds, but they are as gentle as kittens and, big as they are, you'll never get bumped or pushed. The cost for the two-hour experience is $75 per person; age four-seven, $38; children under three, free.

The program is fun, educational and the kids will love it. For more information call 242 373-1244, or simply walk on down to the dock and visit. UNEXSO is an experience all its own.

Guided Tours

Smiling Pat's Adventures

Gilligan's Island Adventure (Mondays and Thursdays)

Of all the activities available to you on Grand Bahama Island, Smiling Pat's day-trip adventure to a tiny, offshore island, the lobster dinner, and the serious fun-in-the-sun that goes on all day long, makes it THE adventure to remember, always.

Smiling Pat

They say a picture's worth 1,000 words. I could not do this trip justice if I used 10,000. I think the pictures in this gallery will tell the tale far better than I could write it.

I will say this, I don't usually go in for adventures such as this one, but I am so glad I did. Pat is a giant of a lady with a giant personality and an even bigger sense of humor, and it's all infectious. The people who work for her, support her and look after her guests are just as much fun as she is. Way to go Pat. Thanks for a great day out, one I'll surely never forget.

Described as, "Grand Bahamas most exhilarating tour experience", no vacation is complete without the Gilligan's Private Island tour! This is a must do!

The adventure starts with a drive to Mclean's Town. From there we'll take a trip by boat to Sandy Cay (AKA Gilligan's Island) for a day of fun on an island all by yourselves!

Gilligan's Island is an uninhabited little islet, complete with coconut trees, pelicans and dolphins. You'll eat lunch, made by the fair hand on Smiling Pat herself, and you'll have some Bahama Mamas and other refreshing drinks (included). Then, if you choose, you can go fishing, snorkeling, go for a swim, or relax and read a book or search for conch shells and leave your name in the sand.

The boat ride out the island is an adventure all its own: a stop along the lends itself for snorkeling over the flat sandy bottom far from the shore, but only a 100 yards, or so from the island. Great times, great adventure.

Adult: $120.00 - Child: $120.00

Grand Bahama West End Tour (Tuesday)

Take a guided tour through The Perfume Factory. The Perfume Factory is located in Freeport's International Bazaar, here you will see how they make their fine island fragrances, sample them and even have the opportunity to buy them!

From there we will head to the local straw markets where you can buy fresh fruit, homemade pepper sauces, and oh so much more! Then we'll go to my Grandmother's M-MMM Good Bakery. She has some of the most wonderful baked goods - coconut bread, banana bread just to name a few.

Then off to Old Bahama Bay for snorkeling, swimming, lounging in the sun and lunch. For lunch, we'll have old fashioned Bahamian "chicken in a bag", fresh Snapper, Conch or Grouper. Oh, and of course, a side of conch salad or peas & rice.

Adult: $75.00 - Child: $75.00

Grand Bahama Beach Tour (Wednesday)

One of the best beach tours in the Bahamas! From beaches with activates to secluded beaches, I will show you the best Grand Bahama Island beaches. The turquoise waters of the Bahama

Islands naturally form some of the most breath taking beaches in the world! Here are a couple of the beaches that we will visit on our beach tour.

Gold Rock Beach

One of the most secluded beaches on Grand Bahama Island! This beach is rated as the top attraction in the Bahamas by Trip Advisor. Gold Rock Beach is the home to many famous movie shoots, including Pirates of the Caribbean II & III. It's located east of Freeport and is secluded within Lucayan National Park. If you can, catch this beach at low tide...it's truly remarkable! While in Lucayan National Park you will discover the pristine splendor of the natural environment on Grand Bahama Island. Walk through the mangroves, admire the wild orchids and other wild flowers as you make your way down to Gold Rock Beach. North of the beach are the Lucayan Caverns, the world's longest underground surveyed cave system.

Taino Beach

During holidays, the beach is the site of many "cook-outs" and is filled with activities for all ages. But times, it will feel like you're own private beach! Taino Beach also hosts the annual Junkanoo Summer Festival. Taino Beach adjacent to Smith's Point Beach, home to the world famous Wednesday Night Fish Fry!

Also on this tour...

We'll stop in Port Lucaya and visit the Garden of the Groves. Here we'll take a walk through the winding trails and see all the beautiful flowers, waterfalls, and sparkling fountains along with some local and migratory birds as well! (There is a $10 fee to get into the Garden of the Groves.)

Adult: $75.00 - Child: $75.00

Smith's Point Fish Fry (Wednesday)

Simply known as 'The Wednesday Night Fish Fry,' this is a party that is held every Wednesday at Smith's Point Beach. Don't miss out on what Lonely Planet has listed as one of the '10 Ultimate Bahamas Experiences'. It is an event that was started by a local church as a way to bring the community together. It's now more than that, it's a favorite of locals and tourists! Let me take you to this weekly tradition so you can try some grouper, lobster and/or snapper, fried up Bahamian-style, along with other specialties unique to the Bahamas. This is a great place to try conch prepared in a salad, as a burger or as fritters. And trust me, everyone's here or on the way. Stick around for after-dinner dancing.(Round trip transportation only)

Round Trip: $20.00

You can reach Smiling Pat directly by sending an e-mail to either pat@smilingpat.com or colleen@smilingpat.com. Pat can also be reached by Phone at (242) 533-2946

East End Adventures (Phone 242-373-6662, eastendsafari@yahoo.com, www.bahamasecotours.com) offers one of the most enjoyable all-day, outdoor experiences available.

This trip to the outback and the east end of the island – 50 miles by road and seven more in a small boat – begins at your hotel when an open 4X4, trailing the boat, picks you up at 8 am. Don't eat breakfast before you leave; you'll get plenty to eat along the way.

The first stop, at about 8:30 am, is **Casuarina Bridge** on the Grand Lucayan Waterway, a man-made canal that cuts the island into two parts between north and south. It was built primarily to enhance the value of the surrounding property. Here, you'll eat a light breakfast of biscuits, muffins and coffee.

From Casuarina Bridge, you'll turn off the main highway and head into a dense jungle of native pine and palm trees to Owl Hole. Along the way, the guides will identify trees and plants used for bush medicines.

Owl Hole, an inland blue hole and home for the past several years to a family of owls, is a short hike from the main trail through dense undergrowth. This is really a large sink hole, and the entrance into an underground, underwater system of caves and caverns connected to the ocean.

After Owl Hole, you'll be treated to a selection of fresh Bahamian fruit: pineapple, mango, melon, grapefruit, and sugar cane. And you'll be introduced to a wonderful local concoction called "gullywash," a strange-looking mixture of gin, coconut water, and condensed milk, seasoned with cinnamon. Whew!

From Owl Hole, if the tide permits, your 4X4 will head for the beach and a ride along the oceanfront to the **Lucayan National Park** (see page 105). There, you'll explore the park, the mangrove swamp, Gold Rock Beach, and you'll feed the barracuda, snappers, needle nose, and a busy little family of ducks. Then it's on the road again to your next stop, McClean's Town, the furthest settlement you will reach by road.

From McClean's Town you head out to sea at great speed in a small boat. Some 20 minutes and seven miles later, you'll land at the dock of the **Fig Tree Restaurant** on Sweeting's Cay, where you'll be met by Ola and Pinna. To describe the Fig Tree as a restaurant is, perhaps, a little misleading. The one-room establishment combines bar, café, and social club all rolled into one. Pinna, the owner, is also the cook, waitress, bartender and general bottle washer. Ola, something of a local celebrity, demonstrates how to extract the conch – part of your lunch – from its shell while your guide picks up the catch of the day. Take a leisurely walk along the seafront, past huge piles of empty conch shells, and watch the crabs fighting among themselves on the sandy bottom of the tiny harbor. Back on the boat and you're off again at high speed to a deserted island for a picnic lunch of conch salad, fresh fish, and a bottle of wine, prepared on the spot by one of your guides. You can stroll the deserted beaches, wade, swim or snorkel in the clear green waters, or just relax under the palms.

After lunch, you'll take to the boat again and, if time allows, skim across the flats, looking for blue holes. When you reach one, you can wade and look into the depths at the hundreds of fish swimming around in the sanctuary of the rocky hole.

Be sure to keep your eyes on the bottom as you go wading; you'll find all sorts of sand dollars, seabiscuits and shells to take home with you.

After the boat ride back to McClean's Town, you'll board the 4X4 once again for the ride back to Freeport and your hotel. By now it's close to 4 in the afternoon, and you're just about ready for another round of gullywash. An hour or so later, you'll arrive back at your hotel, happy, tired and with a whole lot of memories. The cost for all this? Just $110 per person for adults, $55 for kids under 12. $10 discount for cash.

The company also offers the Blue Hole Snorkeling Safari ($85, $35), the Gone Fishin' Safari ($85, $55) and Bonefishing Trips ($250 half-day, $350 full day).

Superior Water Sports

Superior Water Sports in Port Lucaya, Phone 242-373-7863, offers a number of tours in and around Freeport/Lucaya, all well organized, and all at reasonable prices.

1 The **Robinson Crusoe Beach Party** provides lots of fun on the ocean. You'll depart Port Lucaya at either 11 am or noon, depending on the season, on *Bahama Mama*, a 72-foot catamaran, and return either at 4:30 or 5:30 in the afternoon. The first stop is Treasure Reef, where you can snorkel among the coral heads and observe the colorful fish and other marine life. Then it's on to Barbary Beach for a buffet lunch, followed by an afternoon of sunbathing, swimming, and volleyball. There's dancing all the way back to Port Lucaya. The cost for the trip, which lasts about 5½ hours, is $50 per adult, $39 for children under 12, and includes pick-up at your hotel.

2 The **Bahama Mama Sunset Booze Cruise** takes you day-sailing on the 72-foot catamaran, *Bahama Mama*, along the coastline of Freeport to watch, if you're lucky, a magnificent ocean sunset. While cruising, you can dance, enjoy the romantic music, eat a variety of hot and cold hors

d'oeuvres, and drink all the wine and Bahama Mamas you like. You'll depart Port Lucaya at 5:30 and return at 7:30. The two-hour cruise costs $39 per person and includes pick-up from your hotel.

3 **Steak & Lobster Sunset Dinner Cruise & Show**. Sail aboard the *Bahama Mama* for an unforgettable evening of dinner and entertainment. Relax with a complimentary Bahama Mama cocktail before savoring a delicious three-course Bahamian-style dinner of a salad, a steak and lobster entrée (the Bahamian Surf 'n Turf), a choice of desserts, coffee and complimentary wine. Dance under the stars or sit back and enjoy some local live entertainment. The price ($75 for adults, $45 for children under 12) includes transportation to and from your hotel, a full three-course dinner, unlimited Bahama Mama Rum punch and/or fruit punch, free wine all night, live entertainment featuring a Bahamian "Limbo" Show. Mondays, Wednesdays, and Fridays 6:30-9:30 pm, October-March, 6-9 pm, April--September.

Bus Tours

Although there are several bus companies, they all offer much the same in the way of tours and services. You'll also find that most of the major hotels, and some of the smaller ones, have travel desks where you can book your tour. If you wish, you can call the company direct.

Be sure to ask the travel staff at your hotel to show you all that's available; some of them tend to have favorites and will steer you to them if they can.

A **Grand Bahama Day-Trip**, offered by most bus companies, is a great value, and will take you out to the village of West End, the Garden of the Groves, and then back again to Freeport for a look at Millionaire's Row and the city. The cost is $35, which is not bad for the five-hour round-trip.

A bus tour of **Freeport/Lucaya** costs about $19 per person. It takes in all the interesting attractions along the way, including the residential and commercial areas.

A number of operators offer round-trips to the **Garden of the Groves** for about $15. You can find a variety of combinations that include Freeport/Lucaya, the Garden of the Groves, the Rand Nature Center, the Hydroflora Gardens, Lucayan National Park, and more. All you need do is ask any driver.

Boat Tours

The number of tours available on the sea outnumber those on *terra firma.* Once again, your hotel travel desk will be able to point you in a number of directions. All tours include pick-up in the hotel lobby. And you'll need to make sure the hotel staff shows you all that's offered. If your hotel doesn't have a travel desk, drop in at one that does. The staff there will be pleased to help you out, whether you are a guest or not.

You can take a cruise or go on a beach party with **Reef Tours** (Phone 242-375-5880); go sailing on *Tri-wind*, a 55-foot trimaran; take a glass-bottom boat trip on *Mermaid Kitty*; go sailing and snorkeling on the 50-foot *Bright Star*, another trimaran; sail on a 35-foot racing catamaran, the *Lucky Lady*; or board a 50-foot motor yacht and take a snorkeling, lunch and party cruise with **Pat & Diana *Fantasia* Tours** (Phone 242-373-8681). They have a "reef and wreck" party cruise for $40 per person and a "sunset sailing cruise" aboard a 52-foot trimaran for $30 per person. *Island Time*, a 40-foot catamaran docked at the Britannia Pub, leaves twice daily for lunch and booze cruises.

Adventures on Water

Sea Kayaking

Kayak Nature Tours, 140 Seagate Lane, Freeport, Grand Bahama, Phone 242-373-2485; kayaknaturetours@aol.com, www.bahamasvg.com/kayak.html. This outfit offers a comprehensive choice of nature and kayaking tours. Erica Gates and her staff of 10 have many years of experience in the eco-adventure business. They offer short or extended trips, birding opportunities, and much more.

Lucayan National Park Kayak Nature & Cave Tour. $69 Six hours. Safe in any weather – no dangerous creatures. Suitable for all ages; beginners welcomed. Kayaking portion of trip is approximately 90 minutes of light to moderate paddling in inland creek through a mangrove forest. Lunch on private, shady beach. Time for swimming or beachcombing. Guided nature walk and visit to caves. Park entrance fee included.

All Day Water Cay Kayak Excursion. $110 Eight hours – moderately strenuous Kayak through the coastal mangroves to this small inhabited island off the North Shore.

Walk through the quaint native settlement. Visit the church and school and meet the friendly local people. Have a guided nature walk through the hardwood forest, with bird watching. Taste a native lunch of home-baked bread and local specialties.

Peterson Cay Kayak/Snorkel Tour. $79 Five hours. Paddle time to Peterson Cay is about 30 minutes. Peterson Cay is the smallest national park on Grand Bahama and protected from fishing.

Beginners are welcome and both kayak and snorkeling instructions are provided. All equipment is provided. Guides are certified divers and lifeguards and accompany guests throughout the snorkel experience. Snorkel time is about 90 minutes Snorkeling commences from beach on Peterson Cay, giving guests time to become acclimatized and adjust gear After snorkeling a light lunch and beverages are provided on Peterson Cay. Peterson Cay is home to a variety of sea birds some of which are returning to this area for the first time in many years.

Biking Nature Tour. $79 This tour can also be conducted as a day-hike on foot. Tour is five hours – total distance 12 miles. The bike trail goes along the uninhabited south shore and the trail heads through pine forest, wetlands, sandy and rocky shoreline. Stops are made for flora and fauna highlights and picturesque vistas. All equipment is provided. Also included: lunch, snacks, beverages, backpacks and binoculars for bird watching.

Water Cay All-Day Kayak Tour. $150

Water Cay is a remote, tiny island off the north shore of Grand Bahama that can be visited only by shallow-draft boats. Once populated by over 400 people; barely 10 families live on island today. This tour is for experienced paddlers and requires two hours of paddling to the island and two hours return. Part of trip is through challenging mangrove creeks and partly through open water that can be choppy. All equipment, transportation, food, beverages and logistics provided.

Sport Fishing

Grand Bahama is great for sport fishing. The waters are home to many fighting fish, including blue and white marlin, sailfish, bluefin and yellowfin tuna, wahoo, bonito, barracuda, kingfish and dolphin.

Of the many deep-sea operators on the island, you should probably choose from one of the five members of the Charter Fishing Operators Association. They're all pretty well known, both by name and reputation and, while a catch is never guaranteed, you'll get expert advice and guidance. They all charge about the same for their services, and will supply tackle, bait, rods, reels and ice, but not refreshments. The minimum charge per person, for a party of six, is $300 for the half-day (four hours), or $600 for the full day.

Captain Ted Been, Phone 242-352-2797, has a 34-foot Luhrs.

Captain Tony Cooper, Phone 242-352-6782, runs a 38-foot Bertram.

Captain John Roberts, Phone 242-352-7915, at the Running Mon Marina, has a 36-foot Chris Craft.

Captain Doug Silvera, Phone 242-373-8446 (ask to leave a message), in Port Lucaya, runs a 34-foot Hatteras.

Snorkeling & Diving

There are hundreds of opportunities for snorkeling on Grand Bahama and several companies offer snorkeling tours, day-trips, etc.; you'll find them listed on page 119. There are also many exciting dive sites that can be visited with professional operators, who offer a range of services from basic diving instruction for beginners to courses that end in full certification.

UNEXSO

Of all the operators on the island – for facilities, support, and all-around professionalism – UNEXSO, The Underwater Explorer's Society, is the premier outfit. UNEXSO is open to one and all, beginner and experienced diver alike. Even as a beginner, with some basic instruction, you can dive with a pair of Atlantic bottlenose dolphins, visit Shark Junction – where you'll watch and photograph a steel-suited diver feeding the sharks – or you can go wreck and cavern diving. All it takes is a little effort and, in the case of the shark dives, nerves of steel.

For $99, you can learn to dive in a three-hour course and go diving the same day with UNEXSO. They also offer a full range of guided dive options for certified divers, including a three-dive package for $105; a four-dive package for $140, six dives for $210; and nine dives for $315. They also run a two-hour snorkeling trip for $39, departing at 9 am.

In the recent past, they offered a variety of certification courses as well. These have been suspended temporarily, but may be reinstated by the time of your visit. Check with them if you are interested.

Contact: Phone 800-992-DIVE, 242-373-1250, www.UNEXSO.com.

Xanadu Undersea Adventures

Xanadu will teach you how to scuba dive in only three hours, and then take you out to dive over the coral reef. The cost for your first diving adventure with Xanadu is $79. Once you've learned to dive, you can join in single-tank packages from one to nine dives, special night dives, shark dives, and your open water certification.

Contact: Phone 800-327-8150, 242-352-3811, www.nealwatson.com.

Best Dive Sites

The Tunnel

Off Grand Bahama, The Tunnel is named for its swim-through channels. These are populated by large schools of snappers, yellowtails, and jacks.

The Pygmy Caves

The Pygmy Caves are a 65-foot section of the outer reef with a system of caves and caverns running through an extensive formation of coral heads and walls.

Ben's Caverns

A part of the Lucayan Cavern Complex, this is reputed to be the most extensive system of underwater river, cavern and cave systems in the world. The caverns were named for the man who discovered them, Ben Rose, UNEXSO's resident naturalist.

Shipwrecks

There are three shipwrecks off Grand Bahama Island worthy of note. All are accessible with any one of the dive operators on the island.

The *José*

The *José* is a steel-hulled workboat, 45 feet long and 20 feet wide. It had been abandoned and left to rot at the rear of a closed hotel. When the hotel eventually reopened, the new owners asked that the hulk be removed. UNEXO's dive master, Ollie Ferguson, obliged and in 1986 it was towed to its present location. The hulk now sits upright in about 65 feet of water and is an excellent dive for beginners.

The Sugar Wreck

Thought to be the remains of a barge, this is a steel-hulled wreck lying in about 18 feet of water. Lately, it's become home for several large barracuda. The wreckage is pretty well scattered but consists of three fairly large heaps of debris.

Theo's Wreck

Named for the engineer whose idea it was to sink the ship, this is the remains of the cargo vessel, *Logna*. Built in Norway in 1954, it lies on its port side in 100 feet of water. The ship, 228 feet long with a 35-foot beam, is still intact and is a great underwater spectacle. After a long and useful life, the *Logna* was sunk as a joint venture between UNEXSO and her owners, the Bahama Cement Company. The idea was to provide an unusual and exciting diving adventure. Holes were cut in the deck to allow access by divers. The hatches were removed, along with anything else that might pose a danger to an unwary diver, and then the ship was towed out to its present location. It lies off the Silver Beach Inlet on the edge of the Grand Bahama Ledge, where the continental shelf drops off more than 5,000 feet. Theo's Wreck is one of the most photogenic underwater sites in the Bahamas.

Dive Operators

Under Water Explorers Society (UNEXSO)

In business for 33 years, UNEXSO has a staff of 80, with 16 instructors. The company operates seven modern boats with a carrying capacity of 10 to 30 divers. The company's professional affiliations include PADI, SSI and NAUI. The retail store sells a large line of diving equipment, accessories and clothing, and has on hand 60 sets of rental gear. UNEXSO offers diving packages of its own (see page 117), and participates in packages offered by many of the hotels, including the Royal Oasis Golf Resort & Casino, Our Lucaya, the Clarion Atlantik Hotel, the Radisson

Resort on Lucaya Beach, and the Port Lucaya Resort & Marina. UNEXSO has the only recompression chamber on the island. Phone 800-992-DIVE, 242-373-1250, www.UNEXSO.com.

Xanadu Undersea Adventures

In operation for nine years, Xanadu has a staff of 10, with five instructors, and runs three dive boats with carrying capacity for six to 20 passengers. The company's professional affiliations include PADI, SSI and NAUI. Xanadu, in addition to their regularly scheduled dives (see page 117), offers shark dives three days a week and participates with the Xanadu Beach Resort and Marina, and with other hotels on Grand Bahama, in providing a selection of dive packages. Phone 800-327-8150, 242-352-3811, www.nealwatson.com.

Sunn Odyssey Divers

This company operates out of Freeport/Lucaya. It has two dive boats, three guides, and its professional affiliations include PADI and NAUI. Qualified guides will take you on a variety of diving and snorkeling expeditions to the reefs, caves, and wrecks around the island. Phone 242-373-4014, www.sunodysseydivers.com.

Where to Stay & Eat

$	less than $20 per person
$$	$20-$50 per person

$$$ $50+ per person

Dining

Dining is as good as it gets on Grand Bahama, and especially in Port Lucaya. You have to try fresh conch salad.

$$ The Buccaneer is on the beach at Deadman's Reef, almost at the west end of the island. The drive itself is an experience well worth the trip, as is the great European and Bahamian food. The menu includes conch fritters, crabmeat salad, broiled lobster tail, beef tenderloin, wiener schnitzel and rack of lamb, all served in an atmosphere of island greenery. Call Phone 242-349-3794 for reservations and free transportation.

$$ The Captain's Charthouse, on East Sunrise Highway in Port Lucaya, is Bahamian-owned and -managed and, while the menu is definitely aimed at the American visitor, traditional Bahamian specials are available. Conch, lobster, grouper and crab are all served with lavish portions of good old peas and rice. Phone 242-373-3900.

$ Geneva's Place, on West Mall Street, is another of Freeport's authentic island restaurants. The menu is a small one, but includes all the traditional Bahamian dishes, as well as New York strip steak and barbecued chicken. The food is prepared by Bahamian chefs. Their local dishes are spicy and well-seasoned for a flavor that's unique. Phone 242-352-5085.

$ Guanahani's, at the Royal Oasis Golf Resort & Casino in Freeport, is known for its home-smoked dishes. These include smoked chicken, beef and baby back ribs, but that's not all. The restaurant also offers fresh seafood dishes, all with a pronounced island flavor, including conch stir-fry, Bahamian-style pan-fried red snapper with peas and rice, and island lobster tail, split and char-broiled – all at reasonable prices. There's nothing on the menu priced above $19. Phone 242-352-6721.

$$-$$$ Luciano's, located upstairs at the Port Lucaya Marketplace, may be Grand Bahama's most elegant and romantic restaurant. The décor is subtle, the lighting intimate, and the cuisine decidedly French, with just a dash of the islands thrown in. You can dine indoors or outside overlooking the marina. Phone 242-373-9100.

$ The Outriggers, at Smith's Point, just beyond Taino Beach, is a small, very Bahamian restaurant. A fine conch salad and minced lobster are served, along with an appealing assortment of other authentic local specialties. Phone 242-373-4811.

$$$ Pier One at Freeport Harbour, is actually located on and beneath the pilings. The restaurant has many qualities that might persuade you to stop by for a romantic dinner. The food, mostly from the sea, is excellent, though a little pricey. You could watch the sun set in the west, and see the ships as they come and go. However, you're more likely to ignore such mundane, everyday happenings and watch the sharks instead. That's right, sharks. Every evening, just as the sun goes down, the restaurant staff feeds the sharks, and you can watch them do it right from your outdoor table. You'll see sharks lurking in the waters below the restaurant. The menu features a vast collection of seafood dishes, including everything from lobster to lemon shark, and from mahi-mahi to fresh Bahamian stone crab claws. Shark feeding is at 7, 8 and 9 pm. Phone 242-352-6674.

$ The Pub on the Mall, at Ranfurley Circus on Sunrise Highway, is Freeport's oldest and most authentic English pub. The menu includes such British staples as fish and chips, English bangers (sausages), shepherd's pie and steak and kidney pie. The ale, too, is English; John Courage's ale is served either in bottles or on draught. The atmosphere is very casual. It's a great place to mingle. Phone 242-352-5110.

$ Pusser's, in the Port Lucaya Marketplace off Sea Horse Road, claims to be "the place to see, and the place to be seen" on Grand Bahama. Pusser's is another English-style pub. There are large numbers of antiques, model ships, and other nautical memorabilia and artifacts reflecting an establishment you'd more likely expect to find in England, close to the docks in Bristol or Portsmouth, than on a tropical island. The food includes such traditional English dishes as shepherd's pie and fish and chips, along with a pleasing variety of local seafood dishes. Phone 242-352-5110.

$$ Taino's by the Sea, at the Taino Beach Resort & Club, 5 Jolly Roger Drive in Port Lucaya, is one of Grand Bahama's newest restaurants. The atmosphere is French, the waiters are dressed in tuxedos, the décor elegant and intimate, and the food is cooked to order, often at table-side. Specialties include *canard à la bigarade* (roast duckling in a zesty orange sauce), *escalopes de veau "Sirena"* (veal scalopine sautéed in Marsala wine with creamed mushrooms and green noodles), and *filet mignon au poivre noir* (fillet of beef in crushed black peppercorns, pan-fried at the table). Phone 242-373-4677.

$$$ The Rib Room, in the Royal Oasis Golf Resort & Casino on West Sunrise Highway in Freeport, is a quality restaurant, in English pub style. The atmosphere is close and the lights are low. The food is top quality and therefore on the pricey side, but if you like prime rib, the best cuts of steak, and fresh lobster, this is the place for you. Dress is casual, but it would be wise to make a reservation. Phone 242-352-6721.

$$ Ruby Swiss, next to the Royal Oasis Tower on West Sunrise Highway in Freeport, is another elegant restaurant specializing in French cuisine and table-side cooking – a restaurant for gourmets. If you like French food, you'll love their *entrecôte "Café de Paris"* (a strip steak served in garlic butter with a baked potato), *poulet au vin blanc* (sliced chicken in white wine, brandy and fresh cream served with onions and mushrooms), and their famous *fondu "Bourguignon"* (cubes of prime rib dipped in boiling oil right at your table) and served with a sauce of your choice. Phone 242-352-8507.

$$ Scorpio's, at the corner of Explorer's Way and West Atlantic in Port Lucaya, is the oldest restaurant in downtown Freeport. If you like the food of the islands, you're in for a treat at Scorpio's. The Bahamian chefs specialize in cracked conch, steamed grouper, steamed chicken, and minced or broiled lobster. The restaurant is open from 7 am and serves breakfast, lunch and dinner. Phone 242-352-6969.

$$ The Stoned Crab, on Taino Beach, is famed for its fine dining. It's the only restaurant on the island where you can eat right next to the ocean. For more than 20 years the restaurant's exceptional setting and nautical décor have made it an island institution, and a watering hole for locals and visitors alike. Long considered the "in place," The Stoned Crab, with its good food, casual atmosphere, and spectacular views over a moonlit ocean, turns an ordinary night out into something really special. The house specialties include wahoo, yellowfin tuna, swordfish, red snapper, grouper, lobster, stone crab claws, crab cakes and escargots. Phone 242-373-1442.

$ **The Tradewinds Café**, in the Port Lucaya Resort and Yacht Club next to the Port Lucaya Marketplace, is a neat little place where you can enjoy a cup of coffee and a slice of Bahamian cheesecake at lunch time, or a full-blown lobster dinner in the evening. The café's peach melba is a delight, and the Lucayan chicken (marinated in rum, seasoned with sage, roasted with peppers, onions, olives, tomatoes, and served with peas and rice) is out of this world. Phone 242-373-6618.

$$ **Zorba's**, in the Port Lucaya Marketplace, off Sea Horse Road, claims to be the only truly authentic Greek restaurant on the island. Freshly made Greek salads, *tyropitas, spanakopitas, kebabs, moussaka, baklava* and *galatobouriko* are just a few of the treats to enjoy. 242-373-6137.

Accommodations

Old Bahama Bay, some 25 miles west of Freeport, was formerly the Jack Tar Village resort. It has undergone extensive remodeling and renovation over the past several years. Today, it holds its own with any of its more glitzy competitors in Lucaya and Freeport. Set on the oceanfront at the West End of Grand Bahama Island, the complex includes a marina, 47 guest units – cottages and suites – a restaurant, bar, tennis courts, pool, dive shop, and a variety of on-site watersports. The guest units are comfortably furnished, the bathrooms are large and modern, and each unit has its own refrigerator, coffee maker, TV, fax, and Internet connection. The resort boasts more than 25 acres, most of it waterfront, and white sandy beaches. The restaurant – **The Conch Shack** – is open for breakfast, lunch and dinner; the cuisine is Bahamian and American. Old Bahama Bay, West End, Box F-42546, Phone 800-572-5711 or 242-

346-6500, www.oldbahamabay.com. Rates from $260 per night for a double.

Isle of Capri Casino - Our Lucaya, centered upon the two finest beaches on Grand Bahama, is arguably the largest resort in the entire Bahama chain. Lucayan Beach and Taino Beach provide almost eight acres of pristine white sand and some of the most beautiful waters anywhere. The seas banded by the two vast beaches are the perfect setting for a great resort that just about lives up to all the hype that has preceded it.

Our Lucaya today comprises two modern resort hotels – the **Westin at Our Lucaya Beach & Golf Resort**, and the **Sheraton Grand Bahama Resort at Our Lucaya**. The two new Starwood hotels replace two old resorts: the Alantik Beach and the Lucayan Beach Resort and Casino. These two grand old ladies became the media event of the century, at least as far as the Bahamas are concerned, when they were spectacularly demolished several years ago to make way for the new Our Lucaya.

The guest rooms at both hotels, as one might image, are all comfortable, beautifully furnished and come with all modern conveniences. The list of amenities is long and all-encompassing. They provide just about everything you could want to make a vacation memorable: two championship golf courses, three pools, watersports of every description, 14 restaurants, bars and lounges and the newly renovated Isle of Capri Casino at Our Lucaya.

Rivaled only by Atlantis on Paradise Island, Our Lucaya is highly recommended. Rates range from $155 to $490. Sheraton Grand Bahama Resort at Our Lucaya is at Royal Palm Way, Grand Bahama Island, Bahamas, Phone 866-716-8106, fax 242-350-5060. For the Westin at Our Lucaya it's Sea Horse Road, Grand Bahama Island, Bahamas, Phone 866-716-8108, fax 242-350-5060. The website for both resorts is www.ourlucaya.com.

The **Isle of Capri Casino** at Our Lucaya opened on December 15, 2003. The Casino is over 38,000 sq ft with 19,000 sq ft of gaming space. The floor offers more than 350 slot machines in varying denominations, with a high-limit "Jewel of the Isle" room that features $5, $10, $25 and $100 games. There are 49 Game King video poker machines. There are also 33 table games, including craps, roulette, mini-baccarat, black jack, three-card poker and Caribbean stud. There is also a high-limit room for table games players. Phone 1-888-OUR-ISLE. The Isle of Capri website is www.isleofcapricasino.com/Lucaya/ly_gaming.php.

Best Western Castaways Resort & Suites, in Freeport at the International Bazaar, offers a choice of king or double rooms close to the casino action at the Royal Oasis Golf Resort & Casino. Shops, beaches, and watersports centers are only a short stroll away. Rates begin at around $100 per night in the off-season (May to mid-December). Phone 242-352-6682, PO Box F-2629, Freeport.

The Coral Beach Hotel in Lucaya is actually a condominium complex. Consequently, there are never many guest rooms available. The facilities are, however, fairly extensive, and include a swimming pool, one of the best beaches on the island, and **The Sandpipe**r, a popular island night spot. Off-season rates start at $75 per person. Box F-2468, Freeport, Phone 242-373-2468, www.bahamasvg.com/corelbeach.

The Running Mon Marina & Resort, at 208 Kelly Court in Freeport, is located on the water's edge and offers an outstanding array of facilities and organized activities. Guests can choose from a variety of accommodations that include double and king-sized beds. There's also the Admiral's Suite, which has a furnished living room, kitchen, dining area and a Jacuzzi. The hotel's **Mainsail Restaurant** serves both Bahamian and American dishes. They own and operate a glass-bottom dive boat. Guests can enjoy an exclusive evening cruise complete with tropical drinks and the music of the islands. Rates in the off-season begin at $90 per person, per night. Box F-2663, Freeport, Phone 242-352-6834.

The Port Lucaya Resort & Yacht Club, which adjoins the Port Lucaya Marketplace on Bell Channel Bay Road, is only minutes away from the beach. The hotel has its own pool complex and an outdoor Jacuzzi. Guests have a choice of first- or second-floor accommodations, with stunning views of the Marketplace and the marina. You can enjoy a variety of American and Bahamian dishes in the hotel's restaurant. Off-season rates start at around $100 per night, per person. Box F-2452, Freeport, Phone 800-582-2921, www.portlucayaresort.com.

Xanadu Beach Resort & Marina, set on a small peninsula in Freeport, has its own beach and a 72-slip marina. The resort, once the hideaway of legendary recluse, Howard Hughes, offers a variety of first class accommodations and facilities designed to provide an all-in-one vacation. The resort has its own pool complex complete with a bar and poolside service. Watersports of all types are within easy reach, and golfers can play the two PGA-rated courses at the Royal Oasis Golf Resort & Casino. The rooms are comfortable, have been refurnished and redecorated, and all have balconies and tables. Rates begin at $140 per person, per night. Box F-42438, Freeport, Phone 242-352-6783.

Viva Wynham Fortuna Beach Resort at 1 Dubloon Road in Freeport is another of the island's popular luxury resorts. The typical guest at Club Fortuna is young, outgoing, and uninhibited – topless bathing is commonplace. The atmosphere is definitely European – all of the staff members seem to speak Spanish or Italian – and the food includes a selection of Italian dishes. Designed to get you away from the hustle of everyday living, the guest rooms do not have televisions or telephone s, but they are sumptuously furnished and decorated. The rates include three meals per day, and all the windsurfing, kayaking, archery, tennis, and snorkeling you might wish. Rates start at $240 per person, per night. Phone 800-898-9968.

The Deep Water Cay Club is Grand Bahama's most expensive and exclusive sanctuary for members, mostly male, of the corporate world. The club offers its guests (non-members can stay here) an opportunity to relax or fish in an atmosphere of quiet luxury. Each morning, you'll head out for a day's bonefishing or deep-sea fishing. In the evenings you'll relax in the club lounge for a quiet drink, after which you'll enjoy a meal for gourmets in the Club's luxurious dining room. The rustic guest rooms all have ceiling fans and air-conditioning, thick, heavy towels, and embroidered bed linens. Each room faces the sea, and all have porches, umbrellas, and easy chairs; some even have hammocks. Deep Water Cay is located at the east end of the island, almost an hour from the airport, so you'll need to make arrangements with the hotel for a pick up before you arrive. Box 40039, Freeport. $650 per person night, double occupancy, for a minimum of three nights. Deep Water Cay Club is managed by Greenbrier Resort & Club Management Company, ☐912-756-7071, www.deepwatercay.com. The reservation office can arrange for direct charter flights leaving from Fort Lauderdale.

This section serves all the Islands of the Bahamas, including New Providence and Nassau. It's included because much of the information is helpful to visitors with plans to visit places other than Nassau.

Airlines Serving the Islands

Airline Telephone Numbers

Air Canada: ....888-247-2262, www.aircanada.com

Air Sunshine: ....800-327-8900, fax 954-359-8211, www.airsunshine.com

American Airlines: 800-433-7300

American Eagle: ....800-433-7300, www.aa.com

Bahamasair: ....800-222-4262, fax 305-593-6246, www.bahamasair.com

Bel Air Transport: ....954-524-9814, fax 954-524-0115

Chalk's Ocean Airways: 800-424-2857,

www.chalksoceanairways.com

Delta: ....800-359-7664, www.delta.com

Gulfstream (Continental): . 800-525-0280, www.continental.com

Island Air Charters: ....800-444-9904, fax

954-760-9157

Island Express: ....954-359-0380, fax 954-359-7944

Jet Blue Airways: ....800-538-2583, www.jetblue.com

Lynx Air:............................954-491-7576, fax 954-491-8361

Major Air:...........................242-352-5778, fax 242-352-5788

Pan Am Air Bridge: ....800-424-2557, fax 305-371-3259

Sandpiper Air: ....242-328-7591, fax 242-328-5069

Southern Air: ....242-323-6833, 242-300-0155 (toll-free)

Spirit Airlines: 242-377-6150

Twin Air: ....954-359-8266, fax 954-359-8271

USAirways Express: ....800-622-1015, www.usairways.com

Virgin Atlantic: 800-744-7477

Package Operators

American Airlines Vacations: 800-321-2121, www.aavacations.com.

Air Jamaica Vacations: 800-523-5585, www.airjamaicavacations.com.

Apple Vacations: www.applevacations.com.

British Airways Vacations: 800-AIRWAYS,

www.britishairways.com.

Classic Custom Vacations: sold only through travel agents, but you can visit their website at www.classicvacations.com.

Continental Airlines Vacations: 800-301-3800, www.covacations.com.

Delta Vacations: 800-221-6666, www.deltavacations.com.

Liberty Travel: 888-271-1584, www.libertytravel.com.

Tour Scan, Inc: 800-962-2080, www.tourscan.com.

Travel Impressions: www.travelimpressions.com (book through travel agents only).

USAir Vacations: 800-455-0123, www.usairvacations.com.

Vacation Express: 800-309-4717, www.vacationexpress.com.

Charter Airlines - Florida

Dolphin Atlantic Airlines: 800-353-8010, fax 954-359-8009

Trans-Caribbean Air: 888-239-2929, fax 954-434-2171

Resort Charter Airlines

Deep Water Cay Club: 954-359-0488, fax 954-359-9488

Fernandez Bay Village, Cat Island: 800-9490-1905fax 954-474-4864

Great Harbour Cay, Berry Islands: 800-343-7256

Greenwood Beach Resort, Cat Island: 242-342-3053

Hawk's Nest Club, Cat Island: 242-357-7257

Riding Rock Inn, San Salvador: 800-272-1492

Small Hope Bay Lodge, Andros: 800-223-6961

Stella Maris Resort, Long Island: 800-426-0466

Getting There

Nassau/New Providence

Many direct flights are available, as follows: **Air Jamaica** flies from Newark and Philadelphia; **American Eagle**, from Fort Lauderdale, Miami, Orlando and Tampa; **Bahamasair**, from Fort Lauderdale, Miami and Orlando; **British Airways**, from London; **Comair**, from Cincinnati; **Continental**, from Fort Lauderdale, Miami and West Palm Beach; **Delta**, from NY/Laguardia, Boston and Atlanta; **US Airways**, from Philadelphia, NY/Laguardia and Cleveland.

Freeport/Grand Bahama

Direct flights include: **AirTran**, from Atlanta; **American Eagle**, from Miami and Fort Lauderdale; **Bahamasair**, from Miami; **Continental**, from Miami, Fort Lauderdale and West Palm Beach; **TWA**, from NY/JFK.

Getting to Abaco		
Airport	From	Airline
Marsh Harbour	Ft. Lauderdale	Island Express, Gulfstream, Air Sunshine, Bel Air Transport
	Miami	American Eagle, Gulfstream
	Orlando	USAirways Express
	Freeport	Major Air

	Nassau	Bahamasair
Treasure Cay	Ft. Lauderdale	Island Express, Air Sunshine, Twin Air, Gulfstream
	Miami	Gulfstream
	Orlando	USAirways Express
	West Palm Beach	USAirways Express
	Freeport	Major Air
	Nassau	Bahamasair

Getting to Andros		
Airport	From	Airline
Andros Town	Ft. Lauderdale	Island Express
	Freeport	Major Air
	Nassau	Bahamasair
Congo Town	Ft. Lauderdale	Island Express, Lynx Air
	Freeport	Freeport
	Nassau	Bahamasair
Mangrove Cay	Ft. Lauderdale	Island Express
	Freeport	Major Air
	Nassau	Bahamasair
San Andros	Ft. Lauderdale	Island Express
	Freeport	Major Air
	Nassau	Bahamasair

Getting to the Berry Islands		
Airport	From	Airline
Great Harbour Cay	Ft. Lauderdale	Island Express

Getting to Bimini		
Airport	From	Airline
North Bimini	Ft. Lauderdale	Pan Am Air Bridge, Chalk's Ocean Airways
	Watson Island, Miami	Pan Am Air Bridge
	Paradise Island	Pan Am Air Bridge
South Bimini	Ft. Lauderdale	Island Air Charters

Getting to Cat Island

Airport	From	Airline
Arthur's Town	Nassau	Bahamasair
New Bight	Ft. Lauderdale	Island Express
	Nassau	Bahamasair

Getting to Crooked Island		
Airport	From	Airline

Crooked Island	Nassau	Bahamasair

Getting to Eleuthera		
Airport	From	Airline
Governor's Harbour	Ft. Lauderdale	USAirways Express, Air Sunshine, Bel Air Transport
	Miami	American Eagle
	Freeport	Major Air
	Nassau	Bahamasair
North Eleuthera	Ft. Lauderdale	Gulfstream, USAirways Express
	Freeport	Major Air
	Nassau	Bahamasair, Sandpiper Air
Rock Sound	Ft. Lauderdale	Island Express
	Freeport	Major Air

	Nassau	Bahamasair

Getting to Exuma		
Airport	From	Airline
George Town	Ft. Lauderdale	Island Express, Air Sunshine, Lynx Air
	Miami	American Eagle, Bahamasair
	Freeport	Major Air
	Nassau	Bahamasair
Staniel Cay	Ft. Lauderdale	Island Express

Getting to Long Island		
Airport	From	Airline
Stella Maris	Ft. Lauderdale	Island Express, Bel Air Transport
	Miami	American Eagle

	Nassau	Bahamasair

Getting to San Salvador		
Airport	From	Airline
San Salvador	Ft. Lauderdale	Air Sunshine
	Miami	Bahamasair
	Nassau	Bahamasair

Getting to the Turks & Caicos		
Airport	From	Airline
Provo	Miami	American Airlines
	Atlanta	Delta
	Toronto	Air Canada
	Nassau	Bahamasair

Mail Boat Schedules

The following schedules and one-way fares were current at the time of writing but are subject to change without notice. Mail boats leave Potter's Cay, Paradise Island bridge, in Nassau, weekly.

T o	Rou te	Times & Fares
Ab	Marsh	*Miz Desa* leaves Tuesday at

aco	Harbour, Treasure Cay, Green Turtle Cay, Hope Town	5 pm and returns on Thursday at 7 pm. Sailing time is 12 hours. The fare is $45.
	Sandy Point, Moore's Island, Bullock Harbour	*Champion II* leaves Tuesday at 8 pm and returns on Thursday at 10 am. Sailing time is 11 hours. The fare is $30.
Acklins, Crooked Island & Mayaguana		*Lady Matilda*, schedule varies, 242-393-1064. Sailing time is upwards of 15 hours. The fare is $65, $70 and $70 respectively.
Central Andros	Fresh Creek, Stafford Creek, Blanket Sound, Staniard Creek, Behring	*Lady D.* leaves Tuesday at 12 noon and returns on Sunday. Sailing time is five hours. The fare is $30.

	Point	
North Andros	Nichol's Town, Majestic Point, Morgan's Bluff	*Lisa J. II* leaves Wednesday at 3:30 pm and returns on Tuesday at 12 noon. Sailing time is five hours. The fare is $30. *Lady Margo*, leaves Wednesday at 2 am and returns on Sunday at 5 pm. Sailing time is five hours. The fare is $30. *Challenger*. 242-393-1064 for schedule. Sailing time is five hours. The fare is $30.
South Andros	Kemp's Bay, Bluff, Long Bay Cay, Driggs Hill, Congo Town	*Captain Moxey* leaves Monday at 11 pm and returns on Wednesday at 11 pm. Sailing time is 3½ hours. The fare is $30. *Delmar L.* leaves Thursday at 10 pm and returns on Monday at 5 am. Sailing time is seven hours. The fare is $30.
Bimini & Cat		*Bimini Mack*. Schedule varies. 242-393-1064. Sailing time is 12 hours.

Cay		The fare is $45.
Ber ry Island s		*Mangrove Cay Express* leaves Nassau Thursday at 10 pm. Return arrives 7-9 am on Sundays. Fare is $30.
Cat Island , North & South	Arthur 's Town, Bennen's Harbour, Bluff, Big ht	*North Cat Island Special* leaves Wednesday at 1 pm and returns on Friday. Sailing time is 14 hours. The fare is $40.
Cat Island , South	Smith' s Bay, Bight, Old Bight	*Sea Hauler* leaves Tuesday at 3 pm and returns on Monday. Sailing time is 12 hours. The fare is $40.
Ele uthera	Rock Sound, Davis Harbour, South Ele uthera	*Bahamas Daybreak III* leaves Monday at 5 pm and returns on Tuesday at 10 pm. Sailing time is five hours. The fare is $20.
	Gover nor's Harbour & Spanish Wells	*Eleuthera Express* leaves Monday at 7 pm and returns on Tuesday at 8 pm. She also leaves on Thursday at 7 am and returns on Sunday. Sailing time is five hours. The fare is $20.

The Exumas	Ragged Island, Exuma Cays, Barraterre, Staniel Point, Black Point, Farmer's Cay	*Ettienne & Cephas* leaves Tuesday at 2 pm. 242-393-1064 for return. Sailing time is 21 hours. The fare is $50.
	George Town	*Grand Master* leaves Tuesday at 2 pm and returns on Friday at 7 am. Sailing time is 12 hours. The fare is $40.
Grand Bahama	Freeport	*Marcella III* leaves Wednesday at 4 pm and returns on Saturday at 7 pm. Sailing time is 12 hours. The fare is $45.
Inagua		*Abilin* leaves Tuesday at 12 noon and returns on Saturday (time varies). Sailing time is 17 hours. The fare is $70.
Long Island	Clarence Town	*Abilin* leaves Tuesday at 12 noon and returns on Saturday (time varies).

		Sailing time is 17 hours. The fare is $65.
No rth Long Island	Salt Pond, Deadman's Cay, Seymours	*Sherice M* leaves Monday at 5 pm and returns on Thursday (time varies). Sailing time is 15 hours. The fare is $45.
Ma ngrov e Cay	Cargill Creek, Bowen Sound	*Lady Gloria* leaves Tuesday at 8 pm and returns on Thursday at 10 am. Sailing time is five hours. The fare is $30.
	Hatche t Bay	*Captain Fox* leaves Friday at 12 noon and returns on Wednesday at 4 pm. Sailing time is six hours. The fare is $25.
San Salva dor	United Estates, Rum Cay, Cockburn Town	*Lady Francis* leaves Tuesday at 6 pm and returns on Friday. Sailing time is 12 hours. The fare is $40.

Other Sailings

Mail boats also leave Nassau at unscheduled times. You can find out when and for which destinations by calling the Dockmaster's office in Nassau, under the Paradise Island Bridge on Potter's Cay, Phone 242-393-1064.

Abaco

Will Key, Marsh Harbour, 242-266-0059.

Robert Lowe, Hope Town, 242-366-0266.

Maitland Lowe, Hope Town, 242-366-0004.

Truman Major, Hope Town, 242-366-0101.

Creswell Archer, Marsh Harbour, 242-367-4000.

Orthnell Russell, Treasure Cay. 242-367-2570 or 242-365-0125.

The King Fish II, Treasure Cay, 242-367-2570.

Lincoln Jones, Green Turtle Cay, 242-365-4223.

Joe Sawyer, Green Turtle Cay, 242-365-4173.

Trevor Sawyer, Cherokee, 242-366-2065.

Andros

Cargill Creek Lodge, Cargill Creek, 242-368-5129.

Andros Island Bone Fishing Club, Cargill Creek, 242-368-5167.

Nottages Cottages, Behring Point, 242-368-4293.

Bimini

The Bimini Big Game Fishing Club, Alice Town, 242-347-2391.

The Bimini Blue Water Resort & Marina, Alice Town, 242-347-3166.

The Bimini Reef Club & Marina, South Bimini, ☐05-359-9449.

The Sea Crest Hotel & Marina, Alice Town, 242-347-3071.

Weech's Dock, Alice Town, 242-347-2028.

Eleuthera

Coral Sands Hotel, Harbour Island, 800-333-2368.

Valentines Inn & Yacht Club, Harbour Island, 242-333-2080.

Spanish Wells Yacht Haven, Spanish Wells, 242-333-4255.

Spanish Wells Marina, Spanish Wells, 242-333-4122.

Hatchet Bay Marina, Hatchet Bay, 242-332-0186.

Harbour Island Club & Marina, Harbour Island, 242-333-2427.

Exuma

Club Peace and Plenty, George Town, 242-345-5555.

Grand Bahama

Captain Ted Been, Freeport, 242-352-2797.

Captain Tony Cooper, Freeport, 242-352-6782.

Captain Steve Hollingsworth, Freeport, 242-352-2050.

Captain Elon "Sonny" Martin, Freeport, 242-

352-6835.

Captain John Roberts, Freeport, 242-352-7915.

Captain Doug Silvera, Port Lucaya, 242-373-8446.

New Providence

Brown's Charters, Nassau, 242-324-1215.

Captain Arthur Moxey, Nassau, 242-361-3527.

Captain Mike Russell, Nassau, 242-322-8148.

Born Free Charter Service, Nassau, 242-363-2003.

Dive Operators

Abaco

Brendal's Dive Shop International, Green Turtle Cay, 242-365-4411, www.brendal.com.

Dive Abaco, Marsh Harbour, 800-247-5338, fax 242-367-4779, www.diveabaco.com.

Dive Odyssea, Great Abaco Beach Resort, Marsh Harbour, 242-367-3774.

The Hope Town Dive Shop, Hope Town, 242-366-0029.

Walker's Cay Undersea Adventures, PO Box 21766, Ft. Lauderdale, FL 33335, 800-327-8150, www.nealwatson.com/Walkers/WalkersTransportation.html.

Andros

Small Hope Bay Lodge, PO Box 21667, Ft.

Lauderdale, FL 33335, 800-223-6961, 242-368-2014, www.smallhope.com.

Bimini

Bimini Big Game Fishing Club, Alice Town, North Bimini, 242-347-3391.

Bill and Nowdla Keefe's Bimini Undersea Adventures, PO Box 21766, Ft. Lauderdale, FL 33335, 800-348-4644, www.biminiundersea.com.

Bimini Undersea, 242-347-3089.

Cat Island

Cat Island Dive Center, 242-342-3053.

Greenwood Beach Resort & Dive Center, 242-342-3053.

Eleuthera

The Ocean Fox Dive Shop, Harbour Island, 242-333-2323.

Valentine's Dive Center, Harbour Island, 800-383-6480,   242-333-2080, www.valentinesdive.com.

Exuma

The Club Peace and Plenty, George Town, 242-345-5555, www.peaceandplenty.com.

Exuma Fantasea, George Town, 800-760-0700.

Staniel Cay Yacht Club, Staniel Cay, 242-355-2011, www.stanielcay.com.

Grand Bahama

Under Water Explorers Society (UNEXSO),

PO Box 22878, Ft. Lauderdale, FL 33335, 800-992-DIVE, 242-373-1244, www.underwater-explorers-society.visit-the-bahamas.com.

Xanadu Undersea Adventures, PO Box 21766, Ft. Lauderdale, FL 33335, 800-327-8150, 242-352-3811, www.xanadudive.com.

Deep Water Cay Club, Grand Bahama, 242-359-4831, www.deepwatercay.com.

Sunn Odyssey Divers, Freeport, 242-373-4014, www.sunnodysseydivers.com.

New Providence

Bahama Divers, Box 21584, Ft. Lauderdale, FL 33335 800-398-DIVE, www.bahamadivers.com.

Custom Aquatics, Box CB-12730, Nassau, 242-362-1492, www.divecustomaquatics.com.

Dive Dive Dive, 1323 SE 17th St., Ft. Lauderdale, FL 33316, 800-368-3483, www.divedivedive.com.

Diver's Haven, PO Box N1658, Nassau, 242-393-0869, www.divershaven.com.

The Nassau Scuba Centre, Box 21766, Ft. Lauderdale, FL 33335, 800-327-8150, www.nassau-scuba-centre.com.

Stuart Cove's Dive South Ocean, PO Box CB-11697, Nassau, 800-879-9832, 242-362-4171, www.stuartcove.com.

Sun Divers, PO Box N-10728, Nassau, 242-325-8927.

Sunskiff Divers, PO Box N-142, Nassau, 800-331-5884.

Turks & Caicos Islands

Accommodations

Many of these hotels have websites as well. To find them quickly, go to the search engine, www.google.com, and type in the hotel name. If it has a website, the address will come up.

The Abacos

The Abaco Inn, Elbow Cay, 800-468-8799, $120, MAP $33 extra.

The Bluff House Club & Marina, Green Turtle Cay, 242-365-4247, $90, MAP is $34 extra.

The Club Soleil, Hope Town Marina, 242-366-0003, $115, MAP $32 extra.

The Conch Inn, Marsh Harbour, 242-367-4000, $85 EP only.

The Great Abaco Beach Hotel, Marsh Harbour, 800-468-4799, $165 EP only.

The Green Turtle Club, Green Turtle Cay, 242-365-4271, $165, MAP $36 extra.

The Guana Beach Resort, Great Guana Cay, 242-367-3590, $140, MAP $35 extra.

Hope Town Harbour Lodge, Elbow Cay, 800-316-7844, $100, MAP is $33 extra.

Hope Town Hideaways, Elbow Cay, 242-366-0224, $140 EP only.

The Inn at Spanish Cay, Spanish Cay, 800-688-4725, $180 EP only.

Island Breezes Motel, Marsh Harbour, 242-367-3776, $75 EP only.

The New Plymouth Inn, Green Turtle Cay, 242-365-4161, $120, includes MAP.

Pelican Beach Villas, Marsh Harbour Marina, 800-642-7268, $145 EP only.

Schooner's Landing, Man-O-War Cay, 242-365-6072, $150 EP only.

The Sea Spray Resort & Villas, Elbow Cay, 242-366-0065, $150 EP only.

The Tangelo Hotel, in Wood Cay, 242-359-6536, $66 EP.

Walker's Cay Hotel & Marina, Walker's Cay, 800-432-2092, $125, MAP $32-50 extra.

Andros

Andros Island Bone Fishing Club, Cargill Creek, 242-329-5167, call for rates, EP only.

Cargill Creek Lodge, Cargill Creek, 800-533-4353, $275, includes all meals and unlimited fishing.

Emerald Palms by the Sea, Driggs Hill, 800-688-4752, $90, MAP $40 extra.

Green Willows Inn, Nicholl's Town, 242-329-2515, $65, EP only, includes taxes.

Mangrove Cay Cottages, Mangrove Cay, 242-3680, $88 MAP and EP.

Moxey's Guest House, Mangrove Cay, 242-329-4159, $60 EP, FAP.

Small Hope Bay Lodge, Fresh Creek, 800-

223-6961, $150 per person per night, meals and activities included.

Bimini

Bimini Big Game Fishing Club, Alice Town, 800-327-4149, $150 EP.

Bimini Blue Water Resort, Alice Town, 242-347-2166, $100 EP.

The Compleat Angler Hotel, Alice Town, 242-347-3122, $85 EP.

Sea Crest Hotel, Alice Town, 242-347-2071, $90 EP.

Eleuthera

Cambridge Villas, Gregory Town, 242-335-5080, $55, MAP $25 extra.

Coral Sands Hotel, Romora Bay on Harbour Island, 800-333-2368, $160 MAP and EP available.

The Cove-Eleuthera, Gregory Town, 800-552-5960, $110, MAP $38 extra.

Palm Tree Villas, Governor's Harbour, 242-332-2002, $105 EP only.

Palmetto Shores Villas, South Palmetto Point, 242-332-1305, $100 EP only.

Pink Sands, Harbour Island, 800-OUTPOST, $300, MAP $55 extra.

The Romora Bay Club, Harbour Island, 800-327-8286, $160, MAP $38 extra.

The Runaway Hill Club, Harbour Island, 800-728-9803, $125, MAP $40 extra.

Unique Village, North Palmetto Point, 242-332-1830, $90, MAP $35 extra.

Valentines Inn & Yacht Club, Harbour Island, 242-333-2080, $125, MAP and EP available.

The Exumas

Club Peace and Plenty, George Town, 800-525-2210, $120, MAP $32 extra.

Coconut Grove Hotel, George Town, 242-336-2659, $128, MAP $38 extra.

Latitude Exuma Resort, 877-398-6222, George Town, Exuma, from $190.

Palms at Three Sisters, Mt. Thompson, 242-358-4040, $100 EP only.

Peace and Plenty Beach Inn, George Town, 242-336-2551, $130, MAP $32 extra.

Regatta Point, George Town, 800-327-0787, $115 EP only.

Staniel Cay Yacht Club, Staniel Cay, 242-355-2024, $195, includes FAP.

Two Turtles Inn, George Town, 242-336-2545, $88 EP only.

Grand Bahama

Castaways Resort, Box 2629, Freeport, 242-352-6682, $75 EP.

Coral Beach Hotel, Box F-2468, Freeport, 242-373-2468, $75 EP.

Club Fortuna Beach Resort, Freeport, 800-847-4502, $240 EP.

Deep Water Cay Club, Box 40039, Freeport, 242-353-3073, $350 per night for a minimum of three nights.

The Oasis, The Mall at Sunrise Highway, Freeport, Bahamas. 800-545-1300. Rates from $118 through $350.

Our Lucaya, PO Box F-42500, Royal Palm Way, Lucaya, Grand Bahamas. 800-LUCAYAN. Rates from $155 through $490.

Port Lucaya Resort & Yacht Club, Box F-2452, Freeport, 800-LUCAYA-1, $95 EP.

Running Mon Marina & Resort, Box F-2663, Freeport, 242-352-6834, $90 EP.

Nassau-New Providence

The Atlantis on Paradise Island, Paradise Island, 800-321-3000, www.atlantis.com, $325 EP.

Breezes, Cable Beach, 242-327-8231, $200 all-inclusive.

British Colonial Hilton, 1 Bay Street, Nassau, 800-445-8667, www.hilton.com, $200 EP.

The Buena Vista Hotel, Delancy Street, Nassau, 242-322-2811, www.buenavista-restaurant.com/hotel.htm, $95 EP.

Casuarina's of Cable Beach, Box N-4016, 800-325-2525, $105 EP.

The Comfort Suites, Box SS-6202, Nassau, 800-228-5150, $150 EP.

Club Land'Or, Box SS-6429, Nassau, 800-

363-2400, $230 EP.

The El Greco Hotel, W. Bay & Augusta Streets, Nassau, 242-325-1121, $100 EP.

The Graycliff Hotel, Box N-10246, 242-322-2796, Nassau, $170 EP.

Holiday Inn Junkanoo Beach Hotel, Box N-236, Nassau, Phone800-465-4329, $70 to $100.

Nassau Beach Hotel, Cable Beach, 800-627-7282, $125 EP.

Nassau Marriott Resort & Crystal Palace Casino, Cable Beach, 800-222-7466, $225 EP.

The Nassau Harbour Club Hotel & Marina, Box SS-5755, Nassau, 242-393-0771, $90 EP.

Ocean Club Golf & Tennis Resort, Box N-4777, Nassau, 800-321-3000, $280 EP.

The Radisson Cable Beach Casino & Golf Resort, 800-333-3333, www.radisson.com, $180 EP.

Sandals Royal Bahamian, Cable Beach, 888-SANDALS, www.sandals.com, $200 all-inclusive, adults only.

The South Ocean Golf & Beach Resort, 808 Adelaide Drive, 800-228-9898, $140 EP.

Turks & Caicos

I sincerely hope you enjoyed this book. Thank you so much for downloading it.

If you have comments of questions, you can contact me by email. At blair@blairhoward.com I will reply to all emails. And you can also visit my website at www.blairhoward.com to view my blog, and for a complete list of my books.

If you enjoyed the book, I would really appreciate it if you could take a few moments and share your thoughts by posting a review on Amazon.

Other Books by this Author:

Photography Books:

How to Take Better Photographs: Quick and Simple Tips for Improving Your Photographs

Stock Photography: How to take Great Photographs and Sell them Online to Stock Photo Agencies

The Photo Essay: The How to Make Money with your Camera Guide for Writers and Photographers:

Digital Photography - Understanding Composition

Digital Photography – Understanding Focus

Visitor's Guides:

The Visitor's Guide to Bermuda – A Complete Guide to the Islands

The Visitor's Guide to Florida – A Complete Guide to the Sunshine State

The Visitor's Guide to the Bahamas – The Collection (All three books in one)

The Visitor's Guide to the Bahamas – Grand Bahama Island and Freeport

The Visitor's Guide to the Bahamas – The Out Islands: The Abacos, The Exumas, Eleuthera, The Acklins and More

The Visitor's Guide to the Bahamas – Nassau

Civil War Books

Great Battles of the American Civil War - Chickamauga

Touring Southern Civil War Battlefields: From Vicksburg to Savannah

Battlefields of the Civil War – Visitor's Guide

14466902R00090

Printed in Great Britain
by Amazon.co.uk, Ltd.,
Marston Gate.